America Is Headed For A Fall...

by

Ray Douglas

Bloomington, IN   authorHOUSE®   Milton Keynes, UK

AuthorHouse™
1663 Liberty Drive, Suite 200
Bloomington, IN 47403
www.authorhouse.com
Phone: 1-800-839-8640

AuthorHouse™ UK Ltd.
500 Avebury Boulevard
Central Milton Keynes, MK9 2BE
www.authorhouse.co.uk
Phone: 08001974150

First published by AuthorHouse 10/19/2006

ISBN: 1-4259-5039-6 (e)
ISBN: 1-4259-5038-8 (sc)

Library of Congress Control Number: 2006906652

Printed in the United States of America
Bloomington, Indiana

This book is printed on acid-free paper.

Table of Contents

FORWARD

The disasters created by hurricane Katrina, Rita, Wilma, and the other hurricanes of 2005 on the Gulf Coast of the United States should be a wake up call! For some people maybe a *one time* wake up call!

I began this project, for the second time, in early August 2005. I could not find a manuscript that I had began ten or twelve years earlier. I came to the conclusion at that time that no one would listen, so I put the manuscript away and forgot about it. The stock market was at the beginning of the big bubble, the economy was good, we were at peace. Who was interested in warning signs?

Almost like a miracle I found the manuscript in storage in late August, 2005 while I was searching for something else. I believe that some of the old material was better, more to the point at this moment in time, than some of what I was writing a decade later. *That is worth mentioning, things have gotten worse, not better.* The old and the new are now combined in this effort to begin to make a change. What happened on the Gulf Coast, and the behavior of people in New Orleans in particular, is a microcosm of the United States today. Maybe instead of a *wake up* this could be a *last call* in regard to changing some things while, at this moment, there may still be enough time.

It is also a terrific opportunity for a new beginning. Let us not simply relocate these displaced people into the same living conditions in another city or return them to the same conditions as before in New Orleans and on the Gulf Coast. Let's apply the lessons learned in this experience to the broader social problems typified by the disaster on the Gulf Coast in general, New Orleans and the Super Dome in particular. Let's care for the truly sick and the elderly with compassion, but put those capable of working back on their feet! Literally off of their behinds and back on their feet! There will be jobs, provide them with jobs, show them a way out, give them the satisfaction of contributing, give them pride and self esteem, but give them *no more welfare.* Their condition is not their fault alone, it is also the fault of Lyndon Johnson's Great Society and many subsequent decisions regarding our social and welfare systems. We have proved that you cannot successfully simply warehouse people. This is a perfect opportunity to begin to turn things around in that part of the country and the rest of the country. *Let's grab it!*

From this point on most of the material was written before Katrina struck. It is not intended to be grammatically or politically correct. The result is the reality of what time and financial considerations will allow. Please look for the messages, not the mistakes. Professional journalist, reporter or editor I'm not.

In my endeavors as a songwriter and live entertainer I am often described as a storyteller; based on my choice of songs, stories, tall tales, jokes and my own compositions.

Storyteller? Maybe. If so, I hope I am good enough to give this very important story the exposure and attention it deserves.

The following are one man's opinions, written in layman's language as I see it on the subjects that are addressed.

Is America headed for a fall?

What do you think?

CHAPTER ONE
HOW DID WE GET IN THIS MESS?

President Roosevelt, President Truman, and President Eisenhower would, with little doubt, be horrified and furious if they were able to see conditions in America today. Rampant lawlessness, widespread acceptance of misused legal and illegal drug use, gangs roaming the streets armed with hi-tech assault weapons, drive by shootings, carjackings, brutal senseless murders, serial predators raping and killing our children. Great numbers of "fatherless" children born to unwed mothers as young as nine years old, parental child abuse, spousal abuse, partner abuse, unprecedented public vulgarity and disrespect for other people, their property, and their right to a peaceful existence. People insecure in their fortified homes, afraid to leave their homes or walk the streets after dark, home invasions, violent robberies and burglaries. Many fearful of those in authority, few with total confidence in the authorities. Would any one of those Presidents have tolerated such massive degeneration of America on their watch? I think not! This is no reflection on our current President George W. Bush, it has been festering for decades.

1

But what on earth did you expect? If you are a normal average intelligent adult and did not see or expect these things you were either not watching or thinking as the melt down was taking place. Think about it, look back on it as it happened. The signs were there. More than mere "writings on the wall" or "having to read between the lines," the evolution and the events were real, clearly taking place. We all saw the signs, I saw them, you saw them, but few of us did little, if anything, about what we saw and felt. We didn't want to think about or deal with such negative things."It's not my business." "Let someone else do it." "I'm too busy." "I don't want to get involved." "Let the authorities take care of it." Sound familiar? When opportunities were at hand to nip it in the bud we mostly did nothing.

As I see it we have become two Americas. I believe that it is about a toss up between those of us that prefer it the way it was in the pre 1960's days and those who have no respect or regard for others, for traditions, for the law, or precious little anything else, including themselves. There are now several generations of these people who have no other basis on which to form their opinions and beliefs than the ever changing shifting sands since the 1960s. So many that I believe it is necessary to document how it was and suggest how it could be. I am obviously one of the previous to 1960s believers.

I believe that we are being attacked on two fronts. We are being attacked by terrorists and illegal immigrants from outside our country, and our established culture and way of life is being attacked from within by those who have no respect for these values and have no idea what price was paid for this wonderful free way of life. Somebody needs to do something!

I'll try!

But first, a short fairy tale.

Once upon a time there was a big beautiful country where happy people lived. The people had paid a very high price for that happiness, they had just defeated vicious enemies who planned to destroy their country and their way of life The people were historically and predominantly rural people involved in and dependent on agriculture. They grew up knowing that nothing came easy, that it takes hard work and dedication to create a better way of life. They knew of life and death from first hand experience. They saw the fruits of their labor when they harvested a good crop in the fall from seeds they had planted in the spring. They saw their livestock reproduce and flourish when properly cared for. They also saw their crops destroyed by nature and their livestock ravaged by disease, floods, extreme heat and bitter cold. They had witnessed their economic system devastated by hype, greed, and fear. They saw their country attacked without warning while pursuing a path of peace. Still they persisted. It hardened them, tested them. They understood and accepted these facts of life and it provided them with a solid set of values. They knew right from wrong and by-and-large they chose to do what was right.

Their counterparts in the cities were not disconnected from those realities. These city cousins also lived near the land, of necessity they had vegetable gardens, called victory gardens during the WWII, and yards to care for. Most could visit the countryside at will. They bought, processed, marketed and consumed the products of the country people. They too had values based on the same ideals and principles as the people who lived in the country. These city people harvested raw material from the earth, worked in factories, built machinery, automobiles, airplanes, war materials, commodities of all kinds, roads, streets and buildings, did all of the things necessary to create and operate functioning towns and cities. They too had experienced first hand the ravages of war. Both peoples knew that this country was created by struggle and war and that people before them had paid a great price to establish what they now enjoyed. The country was called the United States Of America. The people understood it. They appreciated it. They had recently defended it with their lives.

WORLD WARS ONE AND TWO

I'm going to use the two world wars grouped together as a point of reference, a time and place in the American experience to use as a standard, a place to start. I will attempt to measure what has ensued thereafter against this standard. This is to take nothing away from the brave men and women who fought and died in the Korean, Vietnam, Gulf and Afghanistan wars and other "conflicts." Those would be another story.

I only knew the people of World War One era as *old people*. Civilian and military alike were old people to me when I was a boy. To me they were generally a quiet, modest kind of people. Tempered by war, somewhat freed in spirit and exhilarated by the Roaring Twenties, humbled and hurt by the Great Depression, they appeared to me to understand who they were and what their limitations were. Most were modest, likely to understate their abilities and underestimate their potentials. Kind, considerate, gentle people. Good neighbors.

I'll try to paint a quick portrait in words of these kind of people. In 1972 I sat down with three World War One veterans, one of whom was my uncle by marriage, and a tape recorder. I wanted to record their war experiences first hand, knowing that time was running out on their generation. They are all long since deceased.

One old gentleman was from a well to do family, had attended college and entered military service as a commissioned officer. He took great pride in his position of privilege and then power as an officer. He recounted his memories with sometimes too much detail. None the less he was a real patriot and a good soldier, a gentleman.

He went into a very long story about the Battle of the Arragon Forest. I listened as the bullets zinged, the bombs whistled and screamed overhead, the mortars pounded, and imagined him along with my fine quiet old uncle and the other giant old man as young soldiers with guns in hand blazing their way up a hill engulfed in enemy fire. The old officer relayed, again in great detail and with dignity, his part in the battle. Finally when he finished I asked the other two to tell their stories.

My uncle quietly said that he was just a messenger and that his phone line was cut very early on in the battle. He was alone and operating in a fruit orchard. When his equipment was put out of commission he hid in a hole under a fruit tree, not able or equipped to do anything else as the bullets and bombs and the new dual winged airplanes flew overhead.

I then asked the old giant what he had done. He kind of chuckled and replied "I was asleep in boxcar eleven miles away and missed the whole damned thing!"

That's the way they were. No lying, bragging, making up stories. They just told it as it was. That is the point. No whining, no crying.

Further along in the interview and the war the old officer related that he, the old giant, and some other soldiers were nearly caught in an off limits house of ill repute in Italy by some senior officers. The only avenue of escape was through an underground sewer system that ran beneath the streets and led back to a point near their barracks, which they quickly took. The old officer and the old giant laughed heartily at their great successful out maneuvering of the senior officers. Finally the old giant asked my uncle, with a twinkle in his eye and great delight "Where were you that time?"

With my dignified elderly aunt kind of moved forward on the edge of her chair demurely gazing at the carpet my uncle replied "Oh I was sleeping in my bunk. You woke me up when you came in laughing and making all that racket."

Maybe?

The point of this story is that it is real. The people were unpretending and human. The men defended their country risking their lives, giving their time in the prime of their lives, but never claimed to be heroes, nor did they want or expect that status. The women also did their part to help win the wars, plus maintaining the home while the men were away. Quietly, honorably. Even the off color, possibly embarrassing, house of ill repute part was told without vulgarity, with dignity but humor, with class. Human nature never changes greatly in such matters, but how it is handled does change. Lock this into your brain for later reference.

These people of WW1 and the next generation that followed comprise the backbone of the group of people who rose to the challenges of World War II. The later, it seems to me, awakened to their abilities by the horror and threat of the war, appeared to be somewhat surprised by what they could and did do. They had been humiliated by a painful depression, had been neutral in the face of the nightmare that was raging in Europe and without warning were suddenly thrust into a war on two fronts, in Europe and in the Pacific. They pulled themselves up by their boot straps and fashioned themselves into a creative, intelligent, effective, angry war machine. They volunteered by the thousands for military service, teenagers sometimes lying about their age to qualify. Women and men alike dedicated themselves to one goal, victory, whether they were civilians or in military service. Grandmothers, mothers, daughters, teenagers, housewives and single women became assembly line workers, airplane pilots, truck drivers, WACS and WAVES, doing some work that before the war was performed only by men. They were typified by Rosie The Riveter, the men by G. I. Joe and countless other symbols of their dedication and determination. They were led and inspired by a man they respected, believed in and loved, of course with some notable exceptions. Franklin D. Roosevelt, together with the leaders of the Allied nations, would accept nothing short of unconditional surrender from the Axis powers, Germany, Japan, and Italy. Innocent naive farm boys stepped forward to become tough fighting men, foot soldiers, sailors, marines, merchant marines, highly skilled pilots. Street wise city kids, wise cracking brassy youngsters, lived and fought side by side with the farm boys and girls, small town boys and girls, rich old family college types, you name it. They had a common purpose, a goal to reach. Generally they laid aside their private lives, goals, beliefs, preferences, what-have-you, and worked together to achieve one goal, to win the war.

Make no mistake, their sacrifices were great and uncountable. They gave their time, their blood, their legs and arms and eyes, their fingers and toes, their hearing, their brains, literally, even their very lives to the effort. They sacrificed themselves, their sons and daughters. They gave up necessities and luxuries; sugar, meat, tires, gasoline, you name it. These commodities were needed by the military to win the war, they were rationed to civilians. No new cars or trucks could be bought by civilians. They worked around the clock often without vacations in one great unified effort. They fought, they died, and they won. *Tom Brokaw* aptly called them THE GREATEST GENERATION.

This is a very simplistic synopsis of a very long and complex span of time in American history. It in no way is meant to be anything other than a reference point, a place to start. You could read day and night for the rest of your life and never scratch the surface of the endless stories and accounts of the two wars and the years in between.

It is necessary to point out at this juncture that there are people in America today that have no idea that these wars even happened or that the wars have had any direct effect on their lives. There are people who deny that the wars happened, that what is shown on TV are Hollywood creations. Because of the lack of education on the subject they do not understand that had we not won WWII their grandparents and parents may have been used as slaves or slaughtered, their grandmothers, mothers, sisters and daughters used as sex slaves, beaten and savaged and worked to death, and that they themselves might have been subject to the same treatment if in fact they had even been born. I firmly believe that for this reason alone every child should be required to watch an age appropriate hour on the histories of both wars on the History Channel every school day, starting at the junior high school level.

It seems impossible today to think that we could have lost WWII, that at times it hung in a delicate balance. Except for a few errors in timing and some bad decisions by Adolph Hitler and the Japanese High Command we might very well have been invaded on our own shores with the possible outcome unknown.

This is a very simplistic and brief description of these people, these men and women and what they did. Granted they were psyched by propaganda. Conscripted and volunteer alike they were prepared, if only briefly, by boot camp, schools, academies and an almost endless host of entities to prepare them to fight. The point here is when they were finished they had a uniform look, an attitude, a pride, a direction. When finished they were magnificent, trim, groomed to a T, respectful, confident, unassuming. They know who thy were, what their place was if not what their part was. Tough but gentle, proud but humble.

I want to use an example at this point to portray the grit and attitude of these people, partly for later reference. I had a step brother who's mother was my father's childhood sweetheart. After going separate ways, marrying and raising separate families, our parents rekindled their romance late in life and married. Thus we became adult step brothers. I had heard over the years that this man had been a tail gunner aboard a WWII bomber. I heard that he had flown dozens of missions as such, I don't recall an exact number. That was about all I had ever heard about his experiences in the war. Flat cold facts, no stories, no details, no emotions. His mother told me that he had never talked about it.

I received a phone call at 5:30 AM on the morning of September 10, 1969 at my apartment in Santa Barbara California from my sister. The call was to notify me that my step mother had succumbed to a massive heart attack the previous evening. Linking up with my older brother, who also lived in southern California, we drove to Montana to our dad's home to attend the funeral and burial services, and to spend some time with our dad.

When the services were over, the evening of the funeral was spent at my dad's home. The usual procession of friends and neighbors bringing condolences and plates piled high with home made foods was interspersed with family members visiting and a kind of informal wake. Finally rather late in the evening there began a dividing up of the deceased person's belongings, keepsakes, pictures and such.

In the picture dividing segment this stepbrother airman and I were seated on the living room floor surrounded by a sea of family pictures collected over his mother's lifetime. Among the collection were a few pictures of WWII bombers, B-17s, B-24s, or B-29s as I recall, with groups of very young men around them in various poses. One of the young men, really still a boy, in a picture was quite clearly this now middle aged man seated beside me on the floor. I picked up a picture featuring just him at the back of a giant bomber and gingerly sought to open up a dialog on what he was doing, what all of that had felt like to him at the time it happened. To my great surprise he opened up, of his own volition, and began to talk. I sat transfixed and dumbfounded by what he told me.

He said that he was seventeen years old when he had finished his basic training and that he volunteered for duty in the Army Air Corps. It would be taking liberty with the truth to say that he was a man physically, though he certainly proved to be mentally. He was of average height, maybe five foot eight, and even in his middle years quite fit and trim. In the pictures he was much thinner, his masculine frame not yet filled out and fully developed with muscle. He went on to say that when some of the WWII bombers were first designed and built, they were built with a terrible flaw. In aerial combat it was discovered the hard way that they could be successfully attacked from the rear by faster German fighter planes and shot down. The design of the forward mounted swiveling gun turrets could not defend the rear of the planes from attack, thereby leaving them vulnerable. The solution to the problem was a make-do-modification. The last two or three feet of the cone shaped extreme tail of the planes were cut off, fitted with a bubble like appendage and a machine gun. Due to the aerodynamic design of the aircraft, the tail section was relatively very small, diminishing to a virtual point before being retrofitted with the tail gunner's plastic bubble. The inside dimensions of the tail section were so small that the gunner had to wriggle into position on his belly and lay on his belly operating the machine gun in that posture.

He told me that all tail gunners were volunteers at that time. The volunteers were better suited if the were small and/or thin. He said that the mortality rate was extremely high and that all prospective volunteers were so forewarned. Without braggadocio or macho body language he calmly told me that he had volunteered after being fully briefed about the dangers. He did so because he wanted to do it.

I breathlessly asked how many missions he had flown over France and Germany in that position, and again I believe the number was in the dozens. I asked him why he thought he had survived in view of the facts and statistics. He said that he flew with good crews and gave them the credit. He said he was also just plain lucky. His next statement gives me chills when I think of it to this day. He said, and I quote to the best of my recollection, "I made myself a rule that I never broke. I never started firing my gun until I could see the German's pilot's face!" Unquote. I think he may have said "Or the whites of his eyes," but that was a long time ago and I don't want to exaggerate what he said. In either case I was awe stricken by what I had heard!

My God! Think about it! A fierce looking swastika bedecked German fighter plane bearing down on you at maybe twenty to thirty thousand feet above solid ground with several machine guns aimed at your heavily bomb laden, lumbering, fragile gasoline tank with wings! You on your belly facing maybe the first volley of big bullets and you force yourself to wait until you can see not only the feared Nazi face, but maybe the whites of his eyes! And the man does not think of himself as a hero, he was just doing his job!

Well think what you may, that is my idea of a real hero! There is no prejudice involved in this story, I saw him maybe two or three times before this incident, and never again. These days when I hear the word hero thrown around so loosely I think about that man and the other men and women of those two wars and the ones that followed. There is no comparison between these people and athletes who can run with or pass a football, sink a winning basket, or hit a home run. Superior athletes, maybe, heroes, no.

The United States of America established itself as a world power during WWII. The tyranny of Hitler's Germany in Europe, Africa, Russia and the rest, coupled with the Japanese atrocities in Asia and the Pacific awoke a sleeping giant. At the peak of the war the United States was an awesome industrial complex with a military armed to the teeth, toned, fit, ready for action.

While the combined military forces carried out the actual fighting the people at home, the civilians, made their sacrifices and contributions on a proportionate scale. Men, women and children worked long hard hours in factories of every sort known at that time, turning out the weapons and supplies of war, at the same time producing the goods necessary for the civilian population to sustain themselves and life to go on. Farmers and ranchers, main street businessmen and women, doctors, lawyers, average Joes and Janes pitched in and did their part, plus that little bit of extra that makes the difference. Great war bond drives raised the money needed to make the equipment and supplies to fight, led by big name entertainers, movie stars, politicians, community leaders, and even school teachers. School kids were competing on a weekly basis to bring in the most money the family could raise toward buying a U.S. Savings Bond, a war bond. We envied, and at the same time applauded, the weekly winners. The amounts were small, measured by today's standards. Not thousands, not hundreds, but rather dollars, quarters, dimes and nickels, sometimes a staggering twenty five dollar purchase! But it was ours, us doing our part, and we were proud as hell to do it!

When victory finally came there was enormous relief, jubilation, celebration. There were still a million problems, but the fighting had stopped! The massive slaughter was over. *We* had won!

These collective generations of people had been baptized by fire and world wars the likes of which had never been seen before or have not been seen since. They returned to civilian life and did not want to talk about war or think about war. And they did not talk about it, with relatively few exceptions. Most wanted to live quiet productive lives and "live the American dream." Have a job, buy a home, raise a family. Simple! They had endured so much that they wanted no further conflict. Unfortunately in so doing they planted the seed of problems to come with the following generations that was beyond their imaginations.

CHAPTER TWO

THE SEED

What does a mighty fighting machine do with itself when there is no longer a war to fight? What was our entire nation to do after nearly five years of running at near full throttle when quite abruptly the end came, the goal was achieved, there was no longer a contest, an enemy or a military mission? Remember that America did not start the fight, that we were not on a conquest. We wanted neither the defeated nation's land nor their possessions. We wanted peace.

First, to be sure, there was the cleanup. Bring most of the military personnel home, bring some of the machines of war home, occupy and disarm the enemy.

It is noteworthy at this point to attempt to put the size of the effort into perspective. In the Pacific theater there was a build up of material and machines over the four plus years period so massive that no human mind can possibly conceive it's enormity. To give an example, army Jeeps, weapons carriers, trucks, bulldozers, tanks, all kinds of weapons, machines and equipment were amassed on countless Pacific islands, many with no harbors or loading docks. There was no longer a need or purpose for much of this equipment. In order to recover some of it; perfectly workable and usable Jeeps, trucks, tanks, all of the above mentioned and more were driven and tumbled on top of each other, then more piled atop of those, unit after unit, hour after hour day after day, to build a base in the ocean to be finally finished as a loading dock to retrieve some of the Jeeps, trucks, tanks, etc., etc.. This is a brief description of one dot on a map. Try to envision a map with hundreds, maybe thousands of dots, and then try to convert that into some kind of reality in terms of the massive equipment inventories in the Pacific, in Europe and Africa, to say nothing about what was in America. The mighty ocean going ships and aircraft of all shapes and sizes loaded men, machines, and supplies on board and most of them headed for the ports and air bases of the Allied nations.

Allied military and political leaders labored to hammer out the postwar world design, the administration of justice, the new boundaries, and all of the other details and intricacies related to the destruction of the Axis powers and the reconstruction of their countries as democratic societies.

Again the foregoing is only a mini overview, not intended to describe the actions taking place in that frame of time in any detail. This is only a track to run on to bring the reader into a position to focus on the postwar world, and the United States in particular.

With all of the aforementioned under way, what was the United States to do with the gigantic industrial complex, largely converted to military production and expanded during the war? What would it do with and for the millions of fighting men and women and civilians who would become unemployed when there were no more machines of war to build, no war to fight?

The answers are countless, but for the purposes of this writing I will reduce the matter to effort and result. Feature and benefit.

In a nutshell the factories were converted to produce civilian goods except for those retained to produce postwar military hardware and supplies. Technologies were advancing so rapidly that the very machines that won the war were at the same time becoming obsolete. Production of piston driven engines and airplanes sputtered to a faltering nostalgic trickle as the jets came into their own. Missiles were in their infancy, development a top priority. Aircraft carriers became more important than battleships. The military/industrial complex was well on the way to becoming almost permanent bed partners. The success of the atom bomb set into motion the nuclear age with all of it's threats, fears and urgency. To these efforts a great deal of postwar energy was directed, spurred on by the threat of the imposing Soviet Union. The effort and purpose was to defend ourselves and retain our position as the leading power of the free world. The result and benefit was the development of the means to achieve those goals and that meant jobs. In turn that took up a lot of slack in the conversion of manpower from wartime to peacetime endeavor.

However the big player in the postwar marketplace was the civilian consumer. The average Joe and Jane. Shaken from the doldrums of the Great Depression of the twenties and thirties, energized by the war of the forties, starved by both for consumer goods, the average American went on a buying spree. Everything from candy to new automobiles to new homes, with heretofore only dreamed of conveniences and appliances, could now be bought. The rural electrification of America was under way. Small towns and isolated farms could see the dream of one day having electricity coming true.

17

That in turn brought more gadgets into the mix, washing machines, refrigerators, electric stoves and irons, and lights and radios and welders and electric fences and on and on. And that meant new jobs, more jobs. Along with electricity came natural gas, piped right up to your home for cooking, for heat, hot water and more. And more jobs, new jobs. The horse was giving way to the tractor, the reaper and threshing machine to the combine. More new jobs. The massive demand for, and availability of, new cars created a demand for better roads. New roads. More roads. In turn more and more jobs. At the same time the United States was developing export markets to sell all of these things, and everything else we could dream up develop and build, to the rest of the world.

On top of all of this, and I've only touched the highlights, came the baby boom. And the demand for more products, new products. And unnoticed, buried in all the rush, excitement, accomplishment and achievement was THE SEED. In plain view but unrecognizable to the eye of those predominantly hard working, honest, decent, unaware, almost innocent people, even though they had just been tested by wading through the fires of hell, was THE SEED.

At this point it is necessary to distinguish between the two Americas, the ones who subscribe to and appreciate the beliefs and values set forth so far in this writing, and those who would destroy them, or not care if they were destroyed. All Americans, young and old, who did not and do not buy into the destructive revolution at the heart of the problem are exempted.

It started as a very small movement by a very small percentage of the population, primarily by the youth. It was like a cancer that started small and quietly spread undetected. The WWI and WWII generations busily went about their lives and their new found peace and prosperity and chose not to see it or confront what they saw. They somehow believed that their children would understand what they had gone through and would benefit from the previous generation's terrible experiences. They wanted their kids to have a better life than they had experienced. They were reluctant to confront their kids. They chose to avoid conflict when possible, even at the family level. They made life easy for their kids, many provided too much leisure time and unearned money. They spoiled them. Too many did not teach the kids the value of hard work and money, and did not demand respect for property and the rights of others. This set up the environment in which THE SEED took root.

The American people rolled along through the fifties and early sixties on this wonderful fast moving train, enjoying and capitalizing on the opportunities and bounty at hand. Compared to the Great Depression and the war years this was living in paradise. The teenagers and young adults of this time period generally reflected the attitudes and values of the generations that preceded them. They respected their elders, took pride in working and in their work, their personal appearance, their cars and their accomplishments. Living on the edge was to drive too fast, somehow obtain some beer, smoke cigarettes and chase the one of your dreams. The image of bobby socks, drive in movies and burger joints, and the soda fountain as a gathering place was born during this time. The youth of the fifties were just kind of rolling along with the flow of these times. Young people have always disobeyed their elders, always tested the rules, but it was generally done on a kind of an individual basis, sort of a one-on-one modus operandi, maybe a small group protest here and there. These kids were no different. The boys wore duck-cut hairdos that defied the white sidewall and flat top standards of WWII and the forties. The girls experimented with hair styles and skirt lengths, but nothing far

19

out. The boys drove their customized jalopies and their parents cars a bit recklessly, a little too fast in relation to their experience. A lucky few had new cars. Kids gathered at the drive-ins and soda fountains and thought it was cool. They had a new dance they called the Bop, that was their's alone and cool too. They smoked a lot of cigarettes, that made them feel mature, and that was cool. They managed to procure a few beers or a bottle of wine, maybe some whiskey once in a while. They avoided drinking in front of adults if possible and learned how it feels to throw up your guts in an alley or on a country road. The key here is that they were still accountable to adults. If not their own parents, to the community, to friends, relatives, neighbors. No kid wanted to act or dress or behave in any manner that would make one ashamed if their actions were seen or exposed. It was fine to be individualistic, but never radical. Have a little fun, be a little ornery, a little bit rowdy, but not disrespectful.

Quietly into this mix a new found power evolved. Young people learned that by moving en mass they could push the boundaries of convention. There was nothing new about teenage girls swooning, screaming, fainting and crying over their idols, as an example Frank Sinatra a few years earlier. It was fun and fashionable, the latest rage, silly and looked upon as harmless. Out of nowhere comes a young man that was destined to change everything. But I am getting ahead of myself. First I must explain THE SEED.

THE SEED was not a physical thing. It was a phenomenon created by a series of events that took root in a suitable time and place. All of the necessary elements of nourishment and cultivation developed as the phenomenon itself developed and manifested itself.

A single tiny seed can be plucked from the earth by a bird and have it's promise ended instantly. On the other hand, given a place to root, some light and moisture it will reproduce in the image of the parent from which it came. This is true unless and until some agent of change is introduced at some point in the progression. Left to it's natural development a tiny acorn can become a mighty oak tree, minute by comparison to the giant tree it becomes. At maturity it will have grown a great trunk from which twisted and gnarled limbs support branches that in turn produce twigs that are bedecked with uncountable leaves and finally acorns from which it came. A moderate crushing blow can destroy the promise of an acorn. The same blow would not phase a mature oak tree. This is a perfect analogy of what will hereafter be referred to THE SEED, how easily it could have been controlled early on, and what a massive twisted tangled mess it has produced and become.

The events and resulting conditions briefly described in the previous segments were the germ of THE SEED. A war weary population in the United States dreamed The American Dream and labored tirelessly to make it become a reality. Anyone who wanted to work could find work. That meant they could buy that modest house or build a mansion, relative to their abilities, education, hard work and/ or luck. Every family could have a bit of their own land, a car, undreamed of luxury items and children as desired, so the dream went. And most did. People worked hard to have a "better life" and above all to provide the basis for a better life for their children than they themselves had lived. Sounds great! And it was great! But buried in the mix was the germ of THE SEED.

The fruits of their labor and the comforts created by their toil made these good people feel pacified and content. They had witnessed unbelievable hardship and sacrifice first hand and were content to be home, to have homes and jobs. There was an unspoken trust between them. After all they had stood beside each other through the heat of battle, through the thick and thin of the depression, men and women alike respected and protected their own and each other. In the late forties and early fifties they had a man at the top who could make hard decisions. Harry S. Truman's motto was "the buck stops here!" He was fair, unflappable, non corruptible, outspoken. The people knew where he stood. With him at the helm the majority of the people,with notable exceptions of course, felt secure. He would watch out for them, they could focus on their daily lives and the business at hand.

The germ of THE SEED was the desire to provide better conditions for their children than they had grown up with in their time. The nourishing factor was an unintentional attitude of passiveness regarding the parenting of these Baby Boomer kids. Fathers long absent due to the war had seen enough combat and confrontation to last a lifetime. They were busy working and building and producing material things They naively assumed that their children would think as they thought, want to live the way they were working hard to live. Other dads not so directly affected or involved in the war had developed basically the same attitude by what they had witnessed and experienced, and by osmosis had somewhat the same mind set. Mothers had their shoulders to the wheel as well. Many worked part time, others full time to help provide for the families they dreamed of and produced. As everyone knows motherhood and being a housewife is a full time job in itself, let alone taking on an outside job. Mothers preferred to love and adore their offspring, and they too presumed that children so well provided for and loved would in turn appreciate what had been done to provide such an environment, and in turn become responsible adults. And it worked a good part of the time. The last thing either spouse wanted was to have to confront, correct, spank or otherwise have a negative experience with their own kids if and when avoidable. The nourishment of THE SEED was not a big thing or two, instead it was endless small things, little decisions. Let that pass here, avoid correction there, let Junior have his or her way when the subject was not a big issue. It was OK to spoil the child a bit. Spare the rod here and there. Believe that the child would mature and be able to distinguish between right and wrong.

The fly in the ointment was that the new generations did not have the background and experience on which to base their judgments and make their decisions, that to the generations before them was now second nature. The new generations were beginning to grow up on blacktop and concrete, they had no experience with the grit and the mud and gravel of life. There was an increasing loss of the connection to, and the reality of, natural things and nature. Water no longer came from a spring or a hand pumped well, you turn on a faucet and magically it is there. The need for light was not complicated by the inconvenience of caring for and cleaning a lamp or lantern. Light was at your fingertips with a flip of the switch. Baby Boomers didn't have to walk long distances or care for and saddle up or hook up a horse to go somewhere, school or otherwise. The automobile took care of that, complete with glassed in comfort, "three on the tree, a stove and a jukebox." In "jive" language a column shift, a heater, and a radio.

Homes had a propensity for an invention that was being produced en mass, the television set. It was awesome, it brought entertainment and news of the world right into your own living room. Who needed to go outside to create activity or entertainment? But alas, the TV preferred things to be pretty, romances more flowery than real life, the bad problem solved before the end of the half hour or hour long show. The family garden became an outdated relic, a hobby rather

23

than a necessity, if indeed there was one at all. Food became abundant and inexpensive in packages, cans, frozen, and increasingly fresh due to better modes of refrigerated transportation and display.

It would be all to easy to blame the negative results of all these benefits and improvements on those who received them freely, the Baby Boomers. But consider for a moment that they knew of no other way. In the safe cozy environment of the next ten to twenty postwar years city kids in particular lounged in their homes when not in school, zeroed in on the TV becoming heavier on a diet of Coke, Pepsi, fast food and junk food that the TV promoted. Exercise went the way of the Gooney Bird because fewer and fewer had to chop wood, carry coal, tend the garden or walk to school. Boredom sat in and began to replace the new found joy of the luxurious life. They had nothing to compare their condition to except some ancient history thing their parents harped about, something about a war that happened maybe before they were born, and a Great Depression that was depressing and they did not want to hear about. Many had little or no ties to natural things, no desire to explore and experience first hand on a daily basis. They were secure, but had paid no price for security. They had not sacrificed their time, limbs and lives like the previous generations and it bore little or no relation to their lives and times as they saw it.

These kids were still not in the majority as their teen years came upon them. There was still a majority of good kids from good families who adhered to the ideals and principles of their parents, who knew what hard work was, who had never lost touch with reality and natural things. But in the aforementioned group THE SEED was germinating and the seedling beginning to grow. It was being nourished by indifference, enriched by boredom, watered by ignoring the advice and experience of the elders. The TV was showing these young people a picture of life different than their own experiences, which left them bewildered and confused. Slowly they began to disbelieve, disrespect, distrust. Their parents and teachers, community leaders and authorities should have seen it and recognized it as a dangerous situation. As an acorn or a seedling it could have been controlled relatively easy. On the other hand, in all fairness, the elders had never seen anything like it in their lives.

The outcome of the Korean War added more confusion and disillusionment. Was it a police action or a was it a war? Did we win or lose? Didn't America fight wars to win? As the great power of the free world why did we let our soldiers, sailors, marines and airmen and women die and then settle for a tie, if that is what it was? General Douglas MacArthur had been presented to the people of that era as a great war hero. Suddenly he was removed from his position because he was deemed to be wrong in his prosecution of the Korean war. He retired in somewhat of a state of disgrace, even though he did so with dignity.

Information flew as never before, propelled by the reality of pictures on the TV. Was President Truman wrong it asked? Was he a hard headed bully or a great visionary? Was General Eisenhower really just a man? His pre TV image was much larger than life, yet there he was on TV, in reality only a man. Confusion, suspicion, more nutrition for THE SEED and the sapling.

CHAPTER THREE
MORE FERTILIZER,DISRESPECT

The original element that cracked the walls of convention came in a very handsome package. At first it was shocking, rough cut, unrefined, raw, controversial. Still somehow it was electrifying, fascinating, different. Some loudly proclaimed it to be crude, vulgar. It sang with a new kind of emotion. It shook and vibrated and pulsated and gyrated and danced to a new strong beat. It smiled and snarled. It sported a new controversial length and style of hair. It popularized sideburns. It wore it's own combination of flashy clothes that paled previous swashbuckling movie star styles, and the customary rhinestone and flowery country/western styles. It reinvented the image of guitar players. It insulted the intelligence of the intellectuals, concerned the conservatives, enraged the religious, tantalized television, rocked radio, drove hordes of hysterical teenage girls and young women crazy, made their boy friends and young husbands envious, their mothers and fathers uneasy. IT was Elvis Presley

The youth of the fifties were just kind of rolling with the flow in the pre Elvis days. As stated before, young people have always challenged their elders, always tested the rules. The key here is that they were still accountable to adults. If not their parents, to the community, to friends, relatives, neighbors.

Out of nowhere comes a brash appearing young man with rakish long hair stacked high above long sideburns. He is tall dark and handsome, almost pretty if that can be said about a very masculine man. He was well mannered, a bit shy, and very polite. Unheralded, he quietly arrives in the form of a forty five disk on your local juke box or on the airwaves through your radio. His name is unusual. Friends start to ask if you have heard this or that song. You ask them to repeat the singer's name. "Elvis?" "Elvis who?" "Elvis what?" In the south he is beginning to play joints and the country music venues. He is jeered and applauded, admired and admonished, threatening to some and in turn threatened by some. He had discovered early on, purely by accident, that by gyrating his hips and legs in concert with the music he created a frenzy with girls and young women. He delivered his music with heavy rhythmic beats, new electric guitar sounds, and reverb modified through echo chambers that inspired his young admirers to bump and grind, expressing their own imitations of his movements. Young men and boys tried to imitate him, men and boys still try to this day. Girls and young women became more daring, flamboyant, sexy.

The adults think that it's a fad. It will pass. Some think it's awful. Dyed-in-the-wool country/western radio stations won't play it, it's not country. They say it's too raucous. Elvis Presley doesn't look like the country music stars of the time with their drugstore cowboy hats, fancy custom boots, their own style of western shirts, pants and suits. Rhythm n' Blues stations say he's too country. Ooh-bop-she-bop stations in their infancy don't know what in the heck he is and think they don't care! Easy listener programming don't know that he exists. The popular Hit Parade has fine, finished, polished vocalists: Bing Crosby, Perry Como, Frank Sinatra, a great new natural talent with the right connections named Pat Boone. They love Eddie Fisher, Doris Day, The Ink Spots, The Mills Brothers, just to name a few, and a host of others. Some stations started featuring the new "kid" sounds that Frankie Avalon and other young singers exemplified. The Big Bopper, Jerry Lee Lewis, Little Richard, Bill Haley And The Comets, Buddy Holly are all coming along. So who in the hell needs Elvis?

They all did!

Elvis stood the world on it's ear! As he discovered that he was different he learned quickly to use those differences because people responded. And how! He was an original, an inventor, not a copy cat. As he discovered himself, largely to his own amazement, he discovered that people responded to his originality. He was surprised that what he said that came so naturally to him was so different to others. "Yes Sir." "Yes Ma'am." It caused people to respond in kind. He gyrated, they tried. He curled his lip, they mimicked. He sang, they screamed. He rocked and wobbled and danced, they cheered, applauded, and exploded. Unknowingly he caused a crack in the armor of convention and masses of young people rushed through the opening. They discovered that they could defy convention, their parents, their elders, accepted moral codes, and create a new culture all their own if they acted en mass.

It all seems normal now, pass'e. Back then it was radical, unheard of. Adults gasped and frowned as young girls shrieked and swooned and fainted. Adults watched in disbelief at the phenomenon as hordes of young people clapped and tapped and swayed and jumped and gyrated to this strange new music performed by this unconventional hypnotizing youngster. They watched with astonishment as young women and girls charged the stage, touching him, tearing at his clothes, fighting just to get close to him. Frank Sinatra, with all due respect, never caused that kind of hysteria.

The kids were having a ball! It was all kind of for fun, creating this mob hysteria. And they discovered that they could get away with it! It took policemen to try to control them, how exciting! They drew attention, how gratifying! En mass there was somehow a justifiable way to disobey their parents, the elders, the authorities, their conscience. What freedom! They fed off of Elvis, he fed off of them. It was self generating, perpetual motion. Elvis invented "high energy" performance before there was such a definition of performance. Someone else named it Rock and Roll. Millions have tried to copy it. Nobody has duplicated it!

Referring back to earlier statements, the adults and the establishment saw it but didn't recognize or realize the long term effect it would have. How could they have? Some wanted to do something about it, some tried. Nobody really knew or had any idea about what to do. It was frightening, but up to a point it appeared to be harmless. It was fun, but maybe a little dangerous. There was no law against it, but maybe there should be. Left alone maybe it would just go away!

That was not to be the case. More and more people demanded to hear Elvis' music, and bought his records to prove it like never before. Radio stations responded, played his music, mixed formats so they could, even changed formats. People wanted to see him, hear him, hear about him, learn about him. Newspapers and magazines responded with print and pictures. Movies were planned. Television couldn't resist. His national debut on The Ed Sullivan Show has been a classic from day one, even though his gyrating hips weren't shown.

Those who complained and resisted and admonished couldn't keep the lid on him. He was out of the bottle, and like the proverbial genie, there was no way to put him back!

Men copied his trademark sideburns, standard equipment, if you will. Men's hair became longer. His sometimes almost femme' inspired dress style was imitated by young men, loved by girls and young women. His pink shirts probably inspired pink Cadillacs, Fords, Chevys, Plymouths, Pontiacs, Dodges, DeSotos, even lowly Nash Ramblers. Guitars were the rage.

Entertainers copied, tailored, emulated, used and tried to improve upon his "high energy'" style of performance. They still do. Their performances contributed to the masses of young people rushing through the crack in the wall of convention created by Elvis. Managers and promoters jumped on the bandwagon and contributed. In order to compete Jerry Lee Lewis progressed from kicking his piano stool over to jumping up and "shaking" on the piano itself. Little Richard tried to out jump and out do Elvis with antics and tasteless screaming, insisting that *he* invented Rock 'n Roll. Did he contribute? Yes. Did he invent it? No! Many of the imitations were musically pitiful, but the youth thinking it to be a statement of their generation rewarded it and came to worship it. Much of it was the uneducated playing for the uninformed. But it was new, it was fun, and it was *theirs*! Thousands of guitar playing overnight sensations appeared and disappeared, jumping and gyrating their interpretations to the basic big beat. Allen Freed named it Rock and Roll. Some said it wouldn't last. Others would have been willing to die to see that it would last, some did. Many dedicated their lives to Elvis himself and others to Rock 'n Roll in general. It became an institution with groupies and hippies and grungies and all that good stuff.

Elvis himself would probably turn over in his grave if he were in a clear state of mind and could see what is happening. What would he think about the disrespect that is running rampant today? It is doubtful that he ever had any serious ill intent as a result of the barriers that he broke in his career, and in his day. Could he see a connection between his contribution and the state that America and the world is in today? On the other hand the very freedom that he was so instrumental in creating was also contributory to his own demise.

Colonel Tom Parker, Elvis's manager, saw to it that Elvis' performances were tightly controlled, dished out in doses, withheld, then released. He may have had some control of Elvis's personal life and choices early on in their relationship. Could he have made a difference if his focus had been on the well being of his client instead of on the almighty dollar? We will never know. It is an established fact that The Colonel was fighting demons of his own, big time gambling to name one.

The only people who could have nipped the disrespect for others, for tradition, for the law-and-order phenomenon in the bud were the adults of that time in general, including the appropriate authorities, and the parents in particular. They could have forbidden their youth to be involved with and part of the mass hysteria and lawlessness and counseled them on the subject of idol worship. They could have said a nonnegotiable "NO!" to progressively more offensive hair styles, language, and dress creations that were in poor taste as time went on. They could have stood firmly and united against young women and girls throwing and giving themselves to boys and men in the lime lite. They could have, but didn't, except for a few who found themselves to be in the minority.

So it really wasn't Elvis' fault alone, it really wasn't any one person or group or generation's fault. It just kind of happened. It fed on itself and in turn fed the sapling with the manure of uncontrolled emotion and action.

CHAPTER FOUR
THE LIMBS

With the elements and factors outlined in the previous chapter in place, the fifties rocked on, the sapling grew. The times were a bit sinful and self indulgent, but fun. America was on the move in both physical and mental ways. People thronged to the cities where the jobs and action was, to the south and southwest where the weather was better. This in turn manifested into more freedom from parents and old established behavior expectancy. The connection of people to the land and hard reality stretched a bit thinner. Mavericks on the move!

The effort to stand out, to make a personal statement took on new dimensions. Elvis's comparatively classy big beat music began to sound relatively tame compared to what was coming out of the studios in the early and mid sixties. The background music and beat were brought forth in the mixing to the point where the vocal was frequently of little consequence. In some cases it was literally buried. Years of training, practice and experience were no longer a requirement for becoming an overnight singing sensation. Image was everything, anybody remember Fabian? Poorly prepared "singers" crooned, breathed and shouted their messages, mostly of unrequited love. Guitar players became overnight sensation using new electric guitars and amplifiers and a repertoire of three or four chords using single string notes played to the rhythm of the big beat.

Outrageous hair and dress styles became integrated into the image of the entertainers as part of an acceptable image. Entertainers, their managers, record companies, producers, promoters all zeroed in on the teenagers. The kids were impressionable, excitable, and they had money. They shook the bonds of the stereotype teen with relish and became judges of what was good in music, clothing fashion and behavior, measuring themselves only against themselves, so they thought. Unbeknown to them the commercial interests were quietly orchestrating the show behind the scenes. All that had been so painfully earned and learned before these kids arrived was to be disregarded. All that mattered was what was happening at the moment.

Image creators flourished, capitalizing on the mood of the moment. Somewhere along the way Dick Clark out maneuvered Wink Martindale and other up and coming show hosts with American Bandstand. The contest to have the number one record was openly promoted, even to the extent of buying position, known as "payola." The ever increasing competitive atmosphere required the performers to dress more outlandishly, jump higher, shout louder, become bolder, sexier than the competition.

New dance crazes were the rage. Forgotten was any correlation to one's dance partner. The style was to be more creative than anyone else, including even your partner. New patterns developed by those with no background, talent, education or training on the subject were often primitive, pitiful, plentiful and popular. The blind leading the blind. The self-serving cultural correctness and peer praise of American Bandstand and other shows of that type made them hard to watch for people with cultivated tastes. Kids were coping a self righteous attitude.

Television brought volumes of light to nourish the sapling. Communication flourished as never before spreading the new teen culture throughout America and the world. When a teenager created a new dance idiom and performed it on national TV a backwoods teen could pick it up instantly, and be instantly cool. A far out hair style could be flaunted one day, copied that night, be the new rage the next day. Both TV and radio became braver with lyrics, sexier, brazen, and of course cooler.

Again at this point there could have been some application of restraint by those in broadcasting old enough to know better. Instead, they responded to the teens and their promoters who had the time, interest, energy and money to express their tastes and preferences. Never mind the meek complainers, respond to the roar of the out-of-control kids. Businesses could have controlled what was suitable for sale to some extent. They too instead looked on, looked away and let it happen. And the sapling flourished. It was sprouting strong limbs.

This is not to say that what has been described here is all that was going on. In the heartland, in the east and rural America parents were attempting to raise their kids by their own standards with varying degrees of success. Young people with natural common sense were getting legitimate educations, holding jobs and resisting the temptations that were becoming ever more abundant. Preppy eastern institutions still reflected good values with Ivy League haircuts and clothing styles which were copied and emulated throughout the country. Hillbillies held out, stock brokers stuck it out, ranchers rode it out,statesmen stood against it. Still the wave rolled on, gathering strength. And the sapling grew. The limbs grew stronger.

All wrapped up, the fifties were not all that bad. Starting from the postwar standard, young people worried about nuclear war, evolved with Elvis, danced with Dick, rolled with rock, scrambled into the sixties. The fifties were daring, naughty, fun, exciting, memorable. Maybe more memorable for their fresh creative innocence compared to what has happened since.

The sick sixties literally began and ended with a bang. The presidential election of *John F Kennedy* in 1960 was a bang up affair if ever there was one. Arranged, bought and paid for by his father Joseph P. Kennedy Sr., it was the cohesive that gathered and held America together for a short time.

And what a time it was! A time for hope, of direction, of beauty, of peace , maybe most of all a time of class. The handsome young President, his beautiful young wife, their adorable children and the extended Kennedy family were exactly what the country needed at that moment in time. With this strong and charismatic leader at the helm we felt safe, protected. He carefully and tastefully utilized the family members and their spouses in positions that strengthened and supported his own. Camelot was more than just a stage play, it was brought into everyday life by this young, lively, colorful, eloquent President, his wife Jackie, the children, and the Kennedy family.

"Jack", as he was affectionately called, successfully coerced his younger brother Robert F. Kennedy, "Bobby", into accepting the position of U.S. Attorney General. The two of them appeared to be a "dream team" in fair and equal application and enforcement of the laws of the land. Jack clearly defined his visions and goals, aided no doubt by his experienced but extremely low profile father. Bobby tenaciously labored to achieve those lofty visions and goals. Their ideals were lofty, their opposition well seasoned and entrenched.

Jimmy Hoffa at the head of the mighty Teamsters Union was depicted in the press and on radio and TV as an unscrupulous, shrewd, take-no-prisoners operator. Surrounded by his goons, Hoffa appeared to be untouchable, they said. Whatever it took to retain that position was utilized; threats, extortion, mayhem, murder, they reported. Hoffa and the union became a high priority Kennedy target for reform, we were told.

In Cuba Fidel Castro was conducting himself like the namesake of his type of warfare that had brought him to power, the gorilla. He pounded his chest, made loud threatening noises and feinted runs at the United States. His ties with the Soviet Union were increasing at an alarming rate. A nuclear capability with a missile delivery system was being installed only ninety miles off of our shores in Cuba. President Kennedy was the man in the unenviable seat who would have to make the hard decisions of what to do about this fast growing threat.

When a man is immensely popular and powerful he will automatically have and develop enemies. Jack Kennedy had enemies before he ran for President, developed more as he ran, added to those after he was elected. A branch of the government known as The Central Intelligence Agency was running amok in that time frame, given too much of a free hand due primarily to the fear of a threatening nuclear holocaust. The actions of the "CIA" were cloaked in secrecy; covert operations world wide resulted in everything from manipulations of foreign governments to assassination of their leaders. The Kennedys were concerned and suspicious of this massive agency, it too became an object of justifiable concern and investigation.

At the President's elbow was a man many thought to be of questionable character and integrity, Vice President Lyndon B. Johnson. Thwarted in his drive for the Presidency by Kennedy, Johnson had been selected as Kennedy's running mate, against Kennedy's better judgment and intuition, because of Johnson's ability to deliver votes, and the votes of Texas in particular. Time has revealed that these two men disliked each other more than the expediency of politics at the moment allowed the public to know.

The Kennedys had their strengths and their character flaws, needless to say. No human being is perfect.

Jack's handling of the Bay Of Pigs fiasco in Cuba is a case in point of his strength. The character of the man was forever established because of the way he handled the situation. He faced the nation on national television, admitted his error in judgment and took full responsibility for the failed invasion. No excuses, no blame placed on others, no ducking behind advisers or inaccurate information. No cover up. No delay. He stood up and took the hit.

When faced with tough decisions Kennedy armed himself with the best information he could get, listened to divergent viewpoints and then made his own decisions. He was intelligent enough to seek and listen to the sage advice of his father. Mature enough to consult with and listen to his younger brother Bobby. Tolerant enough to endure J. Edgar Hoover who held a heavy hammer over his head because of the Marilyn Monroe affair and other capers. Above all, smart enough to know all of these things, to recognize that he was human, and in spite of the skeletons in his closet, to do what the people had elected him to do, be President.

The same class and intellect could be said of Jackie. She brought much needed glamor and dignity to the Presidency. She knew the secrets, surely not all of them, she also knew that the Kennedy's personal lives were just that, and how much and what the public should be privy to.

The people of the world living now will probably never know what combination, if any, of the aforementioned combination of elements ended President Kennedy's life, Camelot, and " the dream" with another bang. We are told and asked to believe that it was a nut named Lee Harvey Oswald acting alone for his own reasons. Maybe? Most likely the public will never know much more that we have been told to date. Supposedly there is a time capsule that is to be opened at some date far off in the future. But let's remember, someone knew! If not Oswald, that means that someone may still know!

In any event untold numbers of things ended with those final devastating gunshots. An America that appeared to be intact and on track witnessed on live TV what we thought was impossible. In one minute we believed ourselves to be invincible, in the same minute we were proved to be wrong. Disbelief, shock, horror and indescribable grief settled like a great black cloud over the entire nation and most of the world.

There were many who believed that the Kennedys were dangerously liberal. It could be that they possessed that invaluable sixth sense to know how much liberty is enough and how to rein it in if it becomes threatening or destabilizing. We will never know what the outcome of their ideas, plans, and dreams would have been had

41

they lived. It is clear that they understood that with freedom comes individual responsibility. Referring back to earlier statements about the experience and background required to make sound decisions, it is evident that they were superbly endowed and equipped. However, they may have been too privileged to understand the danger of emancipating masses of people at once, with Civil Rights legislation as an example, who had no such background or experience and were not prepared to know how to handle such dramatic changes and freedoms. Much of what they conceived and started in motion was carried through by LBJ after the death of President Kennedy. Maybe some period of orientation, some more education, some measured steps, some incremental qualifications of some kind would have achieved better results.

Yes, we know that they made mistakes, that they trusted too much, or the bulletproof bubble top would have been in place on the Presidential Lincoln in Dallas and security tighter in a Los Angeles hotel kitchen a few years later. In that sense they were too liberal, too trusting, maybe a split second late on the time to reign it in.

Trust in our fellow human beings took a terrible hit that day, November 22, 1963. Suspicion reared it's ugly head from the lowest street level to the highest government levels. Was it the act of one insignificant man or the result of a massive conspiracy involving maybe even the Soviet Union? Were we being set up for an attack?A takeover, an invasion of our country? The very man who represented the idea of a new beginning for America was stolen from us in an instant. The most powerful man on earth, who we looked to for our individual security and protection, was shot before our very eyes! What the hell would happen next? The elements for the development of the sapling into a young tree were cut loose.

There was something very sinister about the way Lyndon Johnson looked, to me. There was a gut feeling of something misleading when he looked you in the eye through the television camera. Something hollow in the words "My fellow Americuns." Something wrong in the pronunciation. Something questionable about the words "The Great Society." The Great Society for who? Maybe that was it! For who?

The abruptness of the change from the brilliant young visionary of the the New Frontier to the tired old mechanical politics of some dull boring man droning on about the "Great Society" was shocking, almost violent. The impact enormous, immeasurable.

The Kennedys knew that to succeed they had to appeal to the nation's youth. The preceding generations had made their political minds up before the Kennedys arrived on the national scene. They were accustomed to the old ways. It was the old "you can't teach an old dog new tricks" syndrome. So new blood was needed to add to those already in the Democratic Party or Kennedy camp and the Kennedys went out and got the new blood.

These people attracted by the Kennedys did not identify with Johnson. He was almost the opposite of the image they had bought into. The Baby Boomers in general couldn't relate to Johnson. They had watched what they had believed in and held onto blown away. They saw no continuity of purpose and direction in this new President. They thought that there was no future for them, that things had deteriorated into a hopeless state, and all hell broke loose. The strong limbs now supported many branches.

It wasn't LBJ's fault alone, not by a long shot. A phenomenon developed about that time that played right into the hands of disrespect and disorder. Businesses began to take increasingly more advantage of workers, and kids in particular, in the workplace. It was one of the new interpretations of "hey it's not my kid!" Businesses squeezed the kid's wages while increasing the price of the goods and services they sold. Benefits went out the window. Kids started wearing plain white T shirts and plain blue jeans because that was what they and their families could afford. Better, more fashionable clothes simply cost too much. People who would have preferred to dress in good taste were forced to discard their good taste because they couldn't afford it. Young families dressed the little kids the same way for the same reasons. Businesses began to increasingly use a thing called a corporation to shield their investments from the ravages of a business failure by limiting a creditor's recovery to the extent of the assets of the corporation. It was increasingly used and abused. Big corporations becoming richer at the expense of average people. Resentment began changing to distrust and dislike. The haves versus the have-nots. T shirts and blue jeans became the undeclared symbol of the have-nots, and became fashionable, not just necessary. Some called them Blue Jean Babies. Of course the fashion designers jumped on the opportunity and marketed high dollar versions, "fashion jeans." There was a feeling, a sense that something was coming, something was about to happen. The young oak tree was developing twigs on it's branches, it was flourishing.

Another element appeared on the American scene in the early sixties that was to play a huge part in what was to come. I first heard of them when a young Englishman visiting a friend of mine asked me " 'ave you 'eard of the Beatles?". Heavy on the T.

"No," I replied. A picture of Buddy Holly and the Crickets flashed through my brain.

"You will," he retorted smugly. "They're an English Rock group."

I thought to myself, equally smugly, "You don't know the Americans like I do." You see I was in the music business at the time. I knew about our music, about ooh-bop-she-bop, about Ricky Nelson and Apache, about Elvis and our teeny boppers. Well, anyway now you know the rest of the story, as *Paul Harvey* would say. But again, maybe you don't. I'd better continue.

The Beatles were widely heralded, heavily promoted by the time they invaded our musical and physical shores. They did not come up from the bottom here, they started at the top. Their American debut was on The Ed Sullivan Show, the premier variety show of it's time. The Beatles swept the country, border to border, coast to coast in a single night.

They were marvelous, if a bit raw. They were well dressed with good English manners, a touch of English class in their speech and vocabulary, and mops of dark well groomed hair atop their youthful handsome faces. They sang with a sincerity that you could feel, they had a fresh new harmony sound, they played their own instruments and they moved to the big beat. Their music and lyrics were original, creative. English groups openly admitted that they were trying their best to do what the young American musicians were doing. The result was quite different with their English input. Many were instant smash hits in America.

A new wave of very young American girls went wild over the Beatles, they were crazy about them. They swooned and fainted and cried just as the generation before them had done over Elvis and the musical idols of the fifties. The mop top haircuts were the subject of much discussion, but of little concern. America had become accustomed to more hair since the fifties. It was dashing on our handsome young

President and his brothers Who was taking hair as any kind of serious threat?

Fast forward a couple of years. It is now the mid sixties. It is well established by now that crowd control is impossible short of calling out the National Guard if the crowd is large enough. Young people now understand that the same rule applies to what they think, what they say, how they dress, and how they behave. Those who choose to rebel believe that everything preceding their entry on the scene was archaic, old and wrong. Mom became "the old lady," dad "the old man." Respect for everything, including themselves, was not cool. Drugs became cool, loud music, extreme styles of dress, unkempt hair, anything to aggravate the "uncool" adults and the "old school" was the thing to do. They picked up on Hugh Hefner's philosophy espoused in Playboy magazine and took it to a new level that only kids without a moral compass and fueled by drugs could possibly do. Sex, drugs and Rock & Roll began it's long downhill roll as the sixties moved along. The melodic harmonious folk songs of the early to mid late sixties gave way to discord and high volume. Increasingly the uneducated playing for the uninformed masses. Unfortunately it became the new standard for the youth of that time. Those of you who have lived long enough will know this, you do not need to be told. To the rest, this may be a big revelation. For those of you who accepted this as the standard, you might now have some insight on the subject.

The opportunity for adults who cared and those in a position to nip this chaos in the bud came and went during this time. In the south a few politicians made a futile attempt to get some support, to take some positive action. In New York City a few leaders foresaw the coming storm, but got nowhere with their verbal attacks on what they saw as a degeneration of a culture that they valued. And so the small cancer of a few years ago was spreading at a rate beyond the reach and control of the older generations of American people. It was beginning to be exported around the world as the youth of other countries and cultures saw what was happening in America and began their own revolutions.

Example, The Beatles. In a few short years after their fantastic American debut they had degenerated into a drugged out, psychedelic, sorry group of long haired hippie types telling the youth of the world about the wonder of drugs and the drug culture and encouraging them to experiment, to get on board.

What a shame! Just think of what might have been! And those of that time period with no other basis by which to compare still think that The Beatles were wonderful. Some of their music was great and has stood the test of time, no doubt about that. But what they came to stand for and espoused from their bully pulpit and what they lead young people around the world into was disgraceful! Criminal? And the adults kind of looked the other way. Sort of like Nero fiddling as Rome burned. (It may be worthwhile mentioning that Nero later committed suicide. Is there a parallel here?) Kids will be kids if adults do nothing to change their behavior and allow them to be irresponsible.

In the animal kingdom adults keep juveniles in check. From wolves to lions to walruses to elephants this is true. A TV documentary of orphaned elephants in Africa showed that the young orphaned males became rambunctious, aggressive, and came into estrus early when raised in an environment where there were no mothers to teach them, and no senior males present to keep them in check. Upon realizing what was causing the problem, the government moved large dominant males from another preserve into the preserve where the juvenile elephants were harassing people and their crops, harassing and killing rhinos. After adjusting to their new environment the older males took on the juveniles and put them in their place, often following fierce battles. Surprisingly the juveniles in estrus immediately came out of estrus and became docile again under the influence of the senior males. Humans could take a lesson here. Dominant Alpha males in wolf packs put junior aggressive males in their place with a powerful and painful nip on the nose. Dominate female wolves attack junior females viciously when one dares to challenge the status quo. Dominant male lions maul and subdue challengers in fierce battles, sometimes causing injury and even death. The same is true with walruses and other sea creatures. These examples may be too extreme for the human condition, but never the less point out that adult males and females in other species take the effort to keep their young in check through their juvenile years. *Ironically that is exactly what we expect law enforcement to do after human adult supervision, and parental supervision in particular, has been absent or failed and young people are out of control!* Only when they have reached adulthood and have some life experience are young animals able to successfully challenge their elders.

CHAPTER FIVE
DRUGS THE SCOURGE

Remember the tree? The tree might have been any kind of tree to use for this analogy. It could have been a tall straight pine or a spruce, maybe a cottonwood or elm. But the oak was chosen for good reason, because the oak has gnarled, twisted limbs. Some agent of change causes this to happen. I don't know what causes the gnarling and twisting of the oak, but I have an opinion on what the agent was that twisted and gnarled the youth of the sixties and the imaginary tree. That agent was the introduction and wide spread use of drugs.

A massive storm of rebellion was brewing in the mid to late sixties. The "establishment" was largely satisfied with the status quo and chose not to pay attention to the social weather forecasters. I attempted to be a forecaster. I was involved with the young people of that time as their boss, their manager, teacher, friend, relative. We discussed their thoughts, opinions and ideas as they saw them at length, and in one way or another, on a daily basis. I became concerned enough to attempt to analyze what I was seeing and hearing to reduce my conclusions to writing, and to submit those findings to officials at various levels in the State of California where I lived. The responses that I received were uniformly the same. The "officials" assured me that there was no impending threat such as I was suggesting. Everything was under control! The social workers and bureaucrats had a complete understanding of the situation and veritably resented the implication that they could use some outside eyes, ears and viewpoints. There was no interest in street level information. There was no threat of a drug problem.

The magnitude of the gathering storm can be measured by the substantial number and types of elements that were swirling about at the time. A major factor was the unbridled Baby Boomers that are the subject of this particular phase of this writing who were in their teens and early twenties at that time. They were spoiled, bored, poorly equipped to deal with adversity and shielded from individual accountability by acting en mass. They began to believe that they were being used and abused by adults, government, business, and big business in particular. They grouped all of these perceived adversaries together and labeled them "The Establishment."

Many chose to simply drop out. Why work or prepare yourself if there is no hope for the future, the big boom could come at any minute. Why work if there is no hope of getting ahead? Why fight if you have no chance to win? Dropouts with little or nothing to do found a new kind of adventure. Head trips! Drug induced escape from reality. "Beautiful experiences," they said.

The blue jean and T shirt look had a built in advantage. The authorities couldn't establish a profile or an identity by the clothing a suspect was wearing, the generation all looked alike. Unkempt hair and beards further hid identifying features. Sun glasses or "shades" concealed the color and shape of eyes. They also hid the effects of drugs from the viewer. Red, watery, or glassy eyes peered from behind dark lenses but revealed nothing. Enlarged pupils, a sure giveaway, weren't revealed. A new password for the culture was the look; the dress, the hair, the beard, the glasses, the body language. No spoken work was required to communicate that you were hip, cool.

A new word was adapted from an old one to put a label on these people. They thought they were "hip", taken from the old term "hip cat" meaning they were cool, modern, super cool. They were called "hippies."

It was taboo to smile at or speak to a "square" person, especially a "square" stranger. He or she might be a "narc" or an informer. Hippies did smile. When they were high they could project a kind of laid back, glazed-faced-plastic smile. If they were in the happy mode of the high they might sit on the floor, say nothing smile and giggle. Smoking "grass" made them lethargic, it dampened emotion, killed ambition. The new drug of choice for many was "acid", it took them on a trip the nature of which somewhat depended on the state of mind they were in before "dropping" the drug , I was told. If they were in a happy state they might experience beautiful vivid colors swirling about in interesting patterns or beautiful flower fields, as examples. If the acid and their mood created a negative effect it could be a horrible experience, a "bad trip." Acid was dangerous. It was also deadly. They embellished their language with four letter words that were previously rarely spoken in mixed company or in public, especially around women and children. Meanwhile they spoke about love, they sang about it and they made it. It was known as "free love" anybody, anytime, anywhere. The tree of disrespect for authority, decency, and other human beings was producing millions of leaves. Drugs were beginning to disfigure the tree and damage or destroy people of that generation and weaken America.

A faction of American people began to prey on each other's kids like never before. Work them cheap, pocket the extra profit. Sell them drugs, what the hell, "that's someone else's kid". The kids thought of the drugs as recreational, but they sold them to each other to pay for their own. The the suppliers and dealers had a different motivation, BIG money! Men and women alike of legal age seduced teenagers with alcohol, drugs and money. "Free love", in other words sex, was rampant, everywhere. Youngsters left home by the tens of thousands to get in on the action and gathered at liberal tolerant locations. San Francisco California was *the* place to be. They wore flowers in their hair and spoke of peace and love. They wore peace signs and created anarchy. They despised adults, yet derived a living from those they despised the most with as little effort and commitment as possible. Some begged for handouts, sometimes lived on garbage, were homeless, sleeping anywhere they could.

They were in the eye of the storm because they were the eye of the storm. Musicians provided the lightening, wind, fire, and rain that battered and shaped them, but also watered the tree. The Beatles were a classic example. At times they were at the forefront of the charge. They joined the revolution and were accepted, then became a powerful influence. Psychedelic came in, white T shirts out, bell bottoms in, straight legged pants out. New Rock 'n Roll was in, yesterday's songs and singers history. Singers and musicians became increasingly weird, inspired by all kinds of drugs, including the new psychedelic variety. Rewarded for being the farthest out in a contest to see who could be the farthest out, many went berserk. Sheer creeps rose to the top. Uncoordinated clothes and colors became a fashion statement. The tasteless loud noise of the heavy metal bands battered stoned brains. Drug induced prancing, running, jumping and stumbling around on stage was the new form of "high energy" performance. Secret sex and drug messages were concealed in the music, sometimes played backwards to decode. The decibels were increased to promote hysteria, move the masses. Lyrics were repeated again and again to get the message across. It didn't matter, the audiences had a thirty second attention span, anything with a story of any length was too much for the stoned listeners. Every thirty seconds was a new beginning to the rest of their lives. With the lightening flashing, if only from the strobe lights, the wind and rain in their faces, maybe because they had no shelter, they gathered and gained momentum. The drugs, violence, and ferocity of the storm twisted the tree and the generation, creating disrespect and rejection of anything conventional.

Meanwhile, back at the ranch, the winds of change were also blowing. Ever more powerful radio and television stations broadcast this version of the weather news with a passion. Their message penetrated even the most remote geographic areas of America. "Come to the city, that's where the action is," they loudly proclaimed in words and song. "Wear flowers in your hair!" "Throw off the chains that bind you!" "Be hip!" "Be cool!" "Join the love generation!" "Join the sexual revolution!" The subliminal message was if you can't come with us, be like us. Start your own revolution in your own neck of the woods.

We have Playboy Magazine to thank for the main impetus of the sexual revolution. However, the way it was presented and the way it played out were two different things. Hugh and the boys playing in beautiful settings with beautiful young babes was a far cry from grungy hippies doing it in a filthy flop house, or on the grass in a public park on a Sunday afternoon!

Humans have always been reinventing sex. Each individual perceives him or herself to be the world's greatest lover. I know, because I am! But this time around sex was explored and exploited, explained and exhibited, promoted and photographed like never before. In his all knowing capacity Hugh Hefner painted a picture of the gratification achieved through sex so earth shattering that the act itself could be very disappointing, incapable of competing with expectations. Through the illusion of perfect air brushed pictures and poignant words, sex was packaged and glorified to new heights. Carefully chosen young females were paraded as Playmates in bunny suits in the magazine and in the Penthouses. Bunnies never have a headache or PMS or bad breath, they never burp or....well you know the rest. *Marilyn Monroe* may have said it best, words to the effect that in spite of the image she created, she was still only a woman in bed. Maybe that was what *Mick Jagger* referred to when he complained "I can't get no satisfaction," or was he talking about self satisfaction, which has been discussed as a possibility. Who cares? The implication was that if you were rich, successful, intelligent, hip, well read and knew what wine to offer you could ride away to paradise with the Bunny of your choice in your exotic sports car to indulge in surreal sex forever and live happily ever after.

The proof is always in the pudding. Somewhere in his early sixties, at age 62 according to a recent TV special, I'm not sure of the time frame and it doesn't matter, somewhere around 1992, Hefner settled into a marriage and was busy raising babies. Now he is back on the market again since1998, this time with three live-in girlfriends. So which way is it? More confusion, more food for the tree.

Other magazines jumped on the bandwagon and attempted to out Hef Hefner. What most achieved was to cheapen sex in general and women in particular. How low can you go was better as a measure for the limbo dance, not as a standard for pornography. As liberal as he was, as revealing as the pictures were, Hefner somehow presented the cheesy side of life with a touch of class. His contribution was to add wind sheer to the raging storm. The copy cats rode the down draft into the ground.

It has long been known that a woman's best asset is a man's imagination. Hefner and his Playboy Magazine began stripping away, literally, this most valuable asset. Others such as Penthouse, Esquire and the like left nothing to the imagination. Beautiful young women were and are photographed in grotesque poses presenting their most private parts for the whole world to behold. The progression from early Playboy as some sort of art form and forum to a multitude of other just plain gross publications was rapid and appears to be permanent. When freshness and beauty quickly began to wear thin, other forms of photographed sex objects and sex acts began to appear. Kinky shots of well endowed sex kittens, then came harder looking women, add perversion, throw in a male version, bring in children, homosexuals, animals, anything goes! Mixed with some love and respect, sex can be the ultimate in beautiful shared human emotion. It can be fun, exciting and fulfilling just for what it is. It can be disappointing. And it can be just plain ugly!

The illusions of the ultimate sexual experience and enjoyment created by these publications were instrumental in the development of a new kind of hardened human male and female. The male was, in the beginning, pictured as the aggressor, the conquerer, in control, fully aware of his prowess and male superiority. Masculine! He has sometimes regressed, in his lowest form, into a foul mouthed braggart who laps at the heels of women and girls, willing to sacrifice everything for the sexual favors of whoever is willing. He has no class or ego. You see him parading on the cheap TV shows, half to nearly naked, prancing, bragging, begging for sex. He is a pitiful site! He's also popular. People in those shows, and watching those kind of shows, love to see him and themselves in that juxtaposed position. It is also a fact of life in the real world.

His female counterpart has nothing in common with a real lady. The "wuss" believes her sexuality and her ability to perform controls the emotions of any man, that her body is the center of the universe, that by flaunting it's sexual parts in the most flamboyant way she attracts optimum attention. Never mind class, the measure is shock, immediate male response. She is to be pitied.

What the girlie magazines and Playgirl types have never shown are the results of their fantasies and the subsequent human behavior. They never mention the broken homes created by those chasing the fantasies, nor the government supported single moms and their children, nor the diseases spread in the pursuit of the fantasy. Where are the pictures of the "babes" who grew old with a zillion problems, of the people ravaged by the diseases, destroyed by the alcohol and drugs that appeared to be so glamorous?

Of course there are all varieties of those in-between females and males who attract attention in their own way. The youth oriented "now" generations have developed a "to each his or her own" kind of people. Into"self" they project images in their styles that mark their place in time. Babes of the sixties still sport buffont hairdos, hip chicks still part their hair at the top and tuck long locks in behind their ears. Eighties ladies, to use the term loosely in a lot of cases, still look like they have just stuck their finger in a light socket with the electricity turned on. Unfortunately the soft medium length wavy hair prominent in the seventies has nearly disappeared. Soft waves combed or brushed back enhances almost any female face, in my opinion. But it has no shock value. Totaled up, these people reflect their place in time and "self" attitude. As they mature into middle aged adults the "Miz" types rarely smile or say hello in passing. Many men in their fifties and sixties mark their place in time with long gray ponytails, mustaches and beards in various combinations. Tired! Very tired! Hey guys, it's time to be grownups, set a clean cut example for the young people. Your time to revolt has long since passed!

Male and female looked and acted so much alike that chivalry was lost in the process. It's frustrating to have to look for a mustache to determine gender. Case in point. A male friend of mine and I were driving along a city street in our town. As we approached a bicycle rider from behind, pedaling along the right shoulder of the road, I took notice of skin tight speedos and long flowing golden hair. I looked, looked again, hesitated for a moment, then remarked to my friend who was of the age to be interested in such things, "Look at the buns on that babe!"As we passed the rider my friend saw the face before I did and cracked up, laughing uncontrollably. When the face came into view it sported a macho mustache! Oops! It took me a while to live that one down!

The politicians added swirl to the storm. Lyndon Johnson buried us in the Vietnam War using the Gulf Of Tonkin incident, an incident of otherwise little consequence, as an excuse to begin bombing the North Vietnamese. Americans expect to win when they fight a war, even though we settled for less in the case of Korea. In the case of Vietnam we had the technology, the weapons, the people. What we didn't have was the leadership at the top. Granted, there was a high risk of involving Communist China or the Soviet Union, but they were a constant threat either way, whether we fought a limited engagement or an all-out-no-holds-barred Vietnam War. War policy makers fumbled with strategies and essentially dropped the ball. We listened to their devious explanations and double talk and knew that they were not being candid with us. A great grass roots swell rose up against their policies and the war. More compost, more knobs, twigs and leaves on the oak tree.

LBJ had the gall to exchange the silver in our coins for new coins with copper centers and laminated silver on the exterior. He had the audacity to tell us it was somehow to our benefit. That's akin to the bank robber telling the bank teller that the bank will be better off without the money he is taking!

With these combined elements as samples and symbols of a country coming apart at the seams, the sixties ground to a close. The storm gained terrifying momentum and raged across the land. At a point in the development of each of the contributing factors an effective stand could have been made. Allowed to contribute to the storm, the results became virtually unstoppable, of hurricane proportion. In the midst of the storm the oak tree of disrespect and revolt not only survived, the thing prospered, fed and watered by disarray. Near the end of the decade there were big bangs. Robert Kennedy, Martin Luther King and a crew of astronauts surrendered their lives to the bang of the sixties.

The hurricane of the Sixties downgraded to a tropical storm in the Seventies. In the early years peace returned at the price of withdrawal, and in effect defeat, in Vietnam. The massive protests finally conveyed to those in power that a large part of the American population had no stomach for a war that they believed America had no business in to begin with, and wouldn't pay the price to win. Mark one up for President *Richard Nixon.*

Nixon then immediately let us down with the Watergate scandal. He had become so enamored with his successes, which were many, and his power, which was so great, that he believed himself to be invincible. Ten feet tall and bullet proof! We had become accustomed to our elected leaders lying to us, but this one was just too much. Over the top! Too blatant! Even bolder and worse than Johnson before him, *Nixon* faced us on national television and proclaimed "I am not a crook!" However a couple of unbelievably gutsy and highly qualified reporters had the goods on Nixon, and they knew it. At the risk of losing their lives they pursued the evidence that finally persuaded someone who could do something about it to listen and do something. Adios Nixon and company.

This big lie, the attempted cover up, the misuse of power and money, created many new twists and knobs on the tree. The average guy and gal saw that those in the highest positions of responsibility were lying, cheating, stealing, bending the rules, etc., etc..

Monkey see, monkey do! "If the big boys can do it, why shouldn't I?" " They're doing it at their level, I can also do it at mine." Some of our leaders, (who remembers Nixon's first Vice President?) set by example what became the driving force of the continuing storm, dishonesty, more distrust and disrespect. And the oak tree representing the twisted, gnarled tangled human condition became a giant, with drugs embedded in every limb, branch, twig and leaf.

Now try to imagine the Queen Mary out in the open sea filled to the brim with American people of today. They are segregated only on the basis of age. On the lowest passenger deck are babies to age ten, on the next deck are children to age eleven to eighteen only, the next deck up holds young adults nineteen to thirty five, next up middle aged adults thirty six to sixty, out in the open on the top deck are senior citizens sixty one and up. For this demonstration we will assume that there are exactly five passenger decks. The mixture is an equal number representation of today's population by age.

The people on the top deck know that there are problems in the decks below. They speak in hushed tones that something should be done, however they are in the twilight of their lives and prefer to enjoy the cruise and the fresh air and not get involved with what is going on below. They rise early, do their exercises, visit over food and drink through the day. They talk about politics, Social Security, the stock market. They trade stories about their children and grand children, their experiences in life and the weather. They keep an eye on their investments and hope the younger generations will prosper. Their retirement may depend on it! The visits continue through happy hour and an early dinner and many are in bed around 9:00 P.M..

The majority of the middle aged adults on the deck below the seniors are busy wheeling and dealing over cocktails or a beer, making money, planning the next move, except for a few who retired early. Beards, mustaches, goatees and long hair are common. They are upwardly mobile, willing to bend the rules a little to get an advantage. They may dabble in recreational drugs a bit, a little marijuana, a little cocaine, some prefer the more expensive exotics or hard stuff, some even stoop to speed, many wouldn't touch any of it with a ten foot pole. They saw and/or tried all of that when they were kids. For some there is money to be made in the business end of the drug phenomenon. They have no problem with taking advantage of the older folks above them who may depend on prescription drugs or squeezing a few extra bucks out of any of the younger people below. That's business, nothing personal. As far as the stuff going on below is concerned, they are really only interested in it if there is something in it for them personally. If a pretty young secretary is available to accompany the boss on a business trip that's very cool. If not, he may have no problem with finding a hooker, as long as few people know. His wife won't be a problem, she is too busy with her career and shopping as well as running the home in his absence. He's smugly confident that, except for business reasons, she is at home every night. Meanwhile, back at the ranch.... ?

These folks understand that there are gangs, drugs, drug dealers, pimps and prostitutes, rapes and murders and child pornography going on somewhere down there below, but as long as it doesn't come up to level two many will kind of look the other way. Some of the money from those activities might just make it's way up to buy a very nice bottle of wine to share with close friends or a new Hummer, maybe a Beamer, who knows, maybe even a new house in a more prestiges neighborhood. It's all good!

The deck three down from the top has the atmosphere akin to the interior of a living bee hive. These young adults have as the basis for their morals and culture the life styles of their immediate predecessors, the hippie and yuppie generations, especially the "me" generation on the deck just above them. That is what they saw as the grew up, that is the standard on which many base their opinions and ambitions. Of course some do not buy into it but what do they know? Drug use is an accepted way of life, if you so choose, and now it is fashionable to have a cool one in your hand. They do not see themselves as alcoholics, they are simply relaxing with a Bud or a Miller Lite or a Coors or a Merlot. This is how they reward themselves at the end of the work day. Again it's what they saw the adults do when they were kids, how are they to know that it very well may destroy them? All that stuff happens to somebody else anyway. But they take it to a new higher level. It's not some of the time they have a cool one in their hand, it is most of their leisure time, and even when working if possible. A few "squares" gathered over in the corner don't buy it, but their not cool to hang out with anyway. If you are really cool you copy the latest hair styles and clothing trends of the black entertainers and athletes, they are always out front in creating a new look. Never mind that it makes you look ridiculous, it's *trendy* man! Shaved heads, sun glasses, aggressive looking mustaches, goatees, baseball hats on backwards or sideways and a facial scowl along with an intimidating physical stance and some tattoos tells the world you are "bad". The young women of like minded mentality know that to make a sale, meaning to get the male's attention, you must advertise. Number one rule is that you must show all of your body that the law will allow in a given time and place in the most provocative and alluring manner possible. The beach or the grocery store, it doesn't matter, and it will usually get a rise out of the "old folks." It's daring and fun! Toss your hair around, that gets attention. Change the color somehow, to blond if possible, paint your face, fingernails and toenails like the hookers of days gone by. People will notice you, you might even score with your own fifteen minutes of fame on some obscure local TV station or newspaper, if you raise enough hell, maybe bare your boobs in public....

Business and jobs are a necessary evil as a way to support your lifestyle. The motto is get all you can while you can as fast as you can. After all you deserve it, why should you have to wait until you are old like those dinosaurs on deck two! *Roger Miller* (who the hell was he, some playwright that married Marilyn Monroe or something?) sang something to the effect of "Do it unto others before them mothers can do it unto you." So grab all you can quick and don't be too concerned about where it came from. It's pretty easy to dupe those old folks on the top deck, they are a trusting bunch. The ones just upstairs are a little harder, but you are smarter than them and everyone else. As for the ones rolling around in that mess in the decks below, they are young, stupid and vulnerable. When they are old enough to work, work them as hard as possible for as little money as possible. Some will supply them with the drugs they crave and the illegal alcohol that they think is a necessary prop, use them to make money and entertain themselves featuring them in porn movies and websites, maybe score some side benefits. They are oh sooo cute while they are young and there are millions more coming! Take all of that money you can get and buy the biggest, loudest boat money can buy with the least amount of money down, get a giant 4X4 pickup or SUV to pull it and head for the party! Oh, and by the way, pay no attention to those spaced out junkies down the hall who keep the windows closed and the doors locked, some of you can supply their needs upon request.

Parts of deck four look like a nudist camp compared to deck three. In today's modern world you must include boys and girls ages eleven to eighteen in what is referred to as "teens". The girls aren't old enough to understand the effect that running around showing all the skin you can get away with is asking for trouble. Remember that they have seen it since day one of their lives, therefore it is the standard on which they base their behavior. But, like each immediate generation before them, not all but some have taken it to a new higher level. Thongs have replaced bikinis as beach wear for girls, low cut pants and jeans barely conceal pubic hair lines, if the skirts get cut any lower and shorter why even bother, just wear a thong. Boys have picked up on this new level of sexual freedom, some expect and demand performance from the girls. At the moment the latest contest for the younger teenagers is to see which girl can leave her personal identifying color of lipstick farthest up on a boy's penis. What on earth has happened?

We see on television news that some children are beginning to engage in sex at age ten or younger. For some of the teens it is popular for boys and girls to "hook up" for sex without commitment. The girls believe it is cool to "hit" on the boys. Sex in the school or on the bus is daring and currently becoming the rage. Girls performing "blow jobs" on boys is "in." Homosexuality between young girls is no longer shocking or taboo. Thank you very much *Madonna* (who now says her actions might have been over the top, will not let her kids watch basic TV) and Brittany! Great examples! Oh, and the only things separating the genitalia between boys and girls at teen dances are the clothes they wear as they dance "doggie style" in public. Any teen that is interested can learn all about sexual positions and the delights of oral sex by watching Berman and Berman on the Discovery Channel. It has been conveniently on in the early and mid evening hours until recently. And let's not forget to thank MTV for it's cultural contributions. Ditto Girls Gone Wild.

These young people can easily go to other countries if the laws are too strict to suit them in the states, they show you how on TV. You can get crazy, drink until you are loose, irresponsible and vulnerable, get drugs of your choice, and "hook up"if you are even a little bit lucky. The adults have it all set up, really all you need is mom and dad's credit card. Do the adults or anyone else understand or care that there are experienced professional playboys waiting with mouths salivating for the next new crop of girls and young women with hormones raging to show up? Currently the world is stunned and awaiting the latest tidbit of news as the search for Natalee Holloway goes on. What in the hell did her parents think she was going to do in Aruba, lay on the beach and drink Kool Aid? After being irresponsible enough to have allowed her daughter to go in the first place, her mother is now adamantly demanding some positive action from the authorities in Aruba. Her action is typical of many Americans today, somebody else is responsible for my problem! Someone solve it! Fast! The fact that she contributed to the situation big time for allowing her daughter to go in the first place is not even open to discussion. Does it occur to anyone contemplating such a trip that the fact that the laws are different in foreign countries might create cause for concern. It is a big red flag waving in your face, but if you prefer to turn your back you don't have to see it.

Hello! Is anybody out there listening? Letting your "child" go off to a foreign country in order to beat the laws in the USA is playing Russian roulette! Even so, our hearts and sympathies should go out to Natalee and all of the family. Meanwhile back home the stern faced adult news reporters are telling us all on TV how important it is to "protect our children." Double talk! Protect mine for sure, but too many times the attitude is the old "that's somebody else's kid."

Children ages 0 to10 are classified as babies, which in reality they are. They are down on deck five and have no idea what they are in for as they progress upward through the decks. Their minds start out fresh and clean and will be influenced by what they see as they grow. Now there's a comforting thought! They are innocent and totally vulnerable, but fear not! They will be "protected" by the ones in the decks above them. We know that a few of them will be victimized and traumatized by drunks, druggies, pedophiles and repeat sex offenders, but that is the price we pay to have a free society. A few will die in the process, but that is an acceptable percentage! The offenders might be dragged through court, or dragged through court again, maybe not, maybe relocated to a different neighborhood where they will not be so well known.

What? Have we gone completely *crazy?* Totally *raving mad?* We allow this horror to be perpetrated upon our innocent kids in order to protect the rights of adults with altered minds? Is it impossible for rational people to understand that alcohol and mind altering drugs alter minds! Is it not logical that in an altered state of mind the most basic human desires and drives, meaning sex and self indulgence, are foremost on the radar screen of the person under the influence. Should that person not be one hundred percent responsible for his or her actions?

Not so if you watch the high powered criminal defense lawyers on TV plead for lesser sentences for their clients based on the fact that the accused was under the influence of legal or illegal drugs and/or alcohol when the crime was committed.

Look around you! You can easily identify scores of druggies and alcoholics by their looks and actions if you have any basis in reality at all! The spaced out druggies wear their identity boldly out front so others of their ilk can quickly recognize them. Modern day men and women, as well as teenage boys and girls, can readily be seen driving or riding down the street in vehicles with a cool one in their hand. Behold the wino on the street! And of course there are those concealed in casual or professional dress that you would never suspect in a hundred years!

The current official government estimate of Americans using marijuana is seventy million. That is probably a low figure since users do not necessarily volunteer to acknowledge their habit. Think of it! Seventy million people with altered minds wandering around in our midst with who knows what on their minds! The number of people using "meth" in all of it's forms and variations is incalculable. Meth is relatively cheap, easily available, and brings out the worst in people. Anger, all kinds of violence and destruction of property are common as a result of taking the drug. Throw in cocaine, heroin, prescription drugs, alcohol and who knows what else, now someone come up with a number of altered minds in our midst! Does any sane person think we don't have a problem?

Meanwhile the Queen Mary sails on. Everyone knows that she is too big and moving too fast to turn around! All but some of the babies know that "something is wrong" but nobody wants to cancel the cruise, so the party goes on. The ship's owners and crew are enjoying the trip like everyone else. If you listen close you can *hear a rumble*, but no one has the will and fortitude to stop her. She is on automatic pilot. Damn the icebergs! Engines full speed ahead!

Does all of this sound familiar? It is a microcosm of the world we live in today, particularly in the USA. If you don't see it and hear it you are not paying attention! But why do anything, why get involved? It is dangerous to do so! But *I hear a rumble*! You hear people say something has to be done about it, that it cannot continue, that the country is *headed for a fall*. You hear it from a few bright young people, the older the age group, the more your hear it. But who, how, where? Where to begin?

CHAPTER SIX
WHERE TO BEGIN?

It does absolutely no good to whine and complain about a problem or situation if you make no effort to do something about it. There is plenty of that going on regarding the subjects to be addressed. On the other hand doing something about matters this serious has risks and takes time, money, and effort. The solutions offered and suggested will not be in candy coated terms so as not to offend anyone. The political correctness that has been pervasive in America for far too long will find no quarter in this effort to offer some solutions to fix some problems. There is a barrier thrown up around many of the subjects to be discussed that they are "too complex." The problem is not too complex, people, special interests, and politics make the solutions too complex. If man made it, man can fix it! That will be the standard in the approach to suggesting a fix for a problem.

#1

DIG DOWN TO BEDROCK

Dig down to bedrock. What does that mean? If you are going to build a large building or a concrete dam as an example, engineers know that you must dig down through all of the loose or wet material, mud, sand, rocks, rubble, whatever, until you reach solid rock. Bedrock. That solid rock will be the base that your structure is built upon. Failure to do so will, in all likelihood, result in a disaster.

The solid rock to build upon in the human race are the very young children. Forget about changing the generations already contaminated for the moment. Starting with children in the first grade a federal program with standard requirements must be put in place to get these kids off on the right foot. It would continue to closely guide their progress through high school grade twelve. Upon high school graduation every able child would be required to do one year of service to the country; civil service, military service, community service or other entities where help is needed and their abilities could best be optimized. This would go a long way toward solving the problems of indifference, disrespect, property destruction and civil disobedience that we see today. This would teach our youth that nothing is automatic, that it takes effort to build and maintain anything. It would give them some idea of where things come from and what it takes to get them in place for people to use and consume.

We must recognize that integration through busing is largely a failure, that there are cultural differences that cannot be solved by moving children from one place to another. It makes sense to educate them in the area where they live but by a standard equal to all other children in the country, equally administered and enforced. It would obviously have to be administered at the local level with teachers and administrators accountable to federal regulators directly, or possibly the administration could be contracted out to private entities to preclude the effort becoming another inefficient bureaucratic monster, who would monitor results and report to federal regulators. It would turn out to be too much of a hodgepodge if administered at the state level. The standards would be the same from border to border, coast to coast. The same for all children regardless of race, color, or creed. There must be a standard uniform dress code, as an example a white shirt or blouse, blue jeans or skirts, navy blue sweaters if necessary when there is cold weather. The teachers would be required to teach by a federal standard, not what each one personally believes as has happened too much in the past. The basis for the standard would be the principles that this country was built upon. The current concept of No Child Left Behind Behind could be integrated into this proposal to utilize the resources already in place, as it is the concept does not go far enough to solve the problems. For those who choose to not abide by those standards, there is a great big world out there, they're free to go someplace else. If you choose to stay here you choose to abide by the rules, no exceptions.

English would be the primary language, no exceptions. If immigrants want the benefits of this country and our civilization they must expect to integrate into this society. The same goes for the black people, white people, poor people and all others of this country; if you want to participate you must integrate, contribute, do your part. No Ebonics, no excuses based on conditions and customs from the past.

Look at it as a new day, a new beginning. Your child will be guaranteed an equal chance, the same chance that every other child has. No more prejudice because of the clothes you wear, the way you speak or the neighborhood you come from. For people of all divergent races, religions and beliefs, do not expect America to integrate into your culture. If America is to provide the education, the people receiving that education would be required to abide by the rules. No negotiating special circumstances, no excuses, no exceptions.

The educational system in the United States is, on the whole, an international disgrace. I am no soothsayer, but I saw this coming as clear as the sunrise will come tomorrow. As the hippie generation became young adults those so inclined became teachers. Many who were spaced out from their "experimenting" with drugs and had been out to lunch in the years when common sense rubs off on even the most deft of straight youngsters were able to come up with teaching certificates. So equipped they began to preach their philosophies to young and open minds, many of whom were in their years of "experimentation." Talk about putting the fox in charge of the hen house! That's not to say that there were not many fine young dedicated teachers coming on line, but we are talking in the realm of the way a cancer starts out, small but potent. The proper and dedicated school teachers up through the fifties and mid sixties were being replaced by a younger generation typified by long hair and weak spaced out looking eyes, an antiestablishment attitude, and no respect for the long established conventions and standards of the profession. Many of the parents of these students couldn't see it, many or them were seeing through the same glazed eyes.

So began the downward spiral that took the United States from the top of the heap in academic terms to where we have been for sometime, and remain, somewhere near the bottom of the pile. With some anticipatory exceptions, does anyone with common sense and good judgment believe that our current production of high school and college grads can compete with the disciplined and determined minds of the kids coming out of Japan, South Korea, India, China and elsewhere?

This is merely the tip of the iceberg. With female teachers having sex with twelve year old students and college professors the likes of Ward

Churchill, where will it end? The system as it is is broken, it must be fixed. The way to fix it is to go to the operating room, identify the bad material and cut it out. A new controlled and enlightened staff of teachers and administrators with some common sense and discipline will necessarily replace those who are beyond reconditioning and redirection. School boards will have to be purged of members with the "touchy-feely" mentality as will members who have no stomach for the hard task at hand. They may become the new batch of unemployed people to help with the citrus and vegetable harvest, or new employees for the fast food and hotel maid staffs if they are not given a golden parachute as they bail out. So be it! And believe it, when they get hungry enough they will do the work!

The "bowling pin"effect is a very powerful force. When their peers see houses in foreclosure and Beamers going back to the dealerships those who still have teaching jobs might pay a little closer attention to the new job requirements and penalties for non compliance.

#2

STOP THE BLEEDING

The first rule in the emergency room is to stop the bleeding. This makes a crystal clear analogy when applied to the critical conditions that exist in the United States today. Stop throwing tax money away trying to rehabilitate chronic alcoholics, drug users and offenders, dealers and career criminals of all kinds and descriptions. Perform immediate exploratory surgery! Determine what is salvageable and what must be removed and discarded. This means in effect that people from several generations who refuse to live by a very clear and concise set of rules and laws must be regarded as incorrigibles. It should never be government policy to support and enable people who choose to ruin their lives with drugs and alcohol, and prey on others to support their habits, as an example. They made their choices, they made their bed, let them sleep in it. If we stop making it comfortable with government sponsored welfare and rehab centers and halfway houses and endless other "poor baby" programs the reality of the misery might open some eyes and minds. If not, "oh well."

Millions of people who are capable of supporting themselves must be removed from the welfare roles. If they can contribute to their support in any way they should be required to do so. This would begin to solve a myriad of problems. Example. People with nothing but time on their hands easily fall into the traps of drugs and crime out of sheer boredom. There is too often no incentive to work or create something or achieve something if you have a welfare check and food stamps coming on a regular basis. Instead of hanging around conspiring ways to beat and cheat the system and supplementing their welfare checks with drug sales, robberies and burglaries, their minds and hands would be focused on the job at hand and the gnawing in their stomachs like those who work every day. If they were required to keep busy they would build up some self pride and self esteem from what they accomplish. They may or may not like or enjoy the work, but after missing a few meals it might look much better than the alternative. That in return would help to relieve the labor shortage that makes coming to the USA so attractive to the Mexican people and other foreigners who risk their lives to gladly perform work that is beneath the dignity of the welfare recipients who are capable of working.

#3

MAKE THE PUNISHMENT FIT THE CRIME

Make the punishment fit the crime! No exceptions! An eye for an eye, a tooth for a tooth! This has all been worked in other places and other times, but America and the world generally has gone soft on crime. Over time the "touchy-feely" philosophy overtook the experience and common sense of other people and other generations who understood that the punishment must fit the crime. The thinking is that somehow you can convert and save everyone, that capital punishment is cruel and unusual punishment not fit for our modern day way of thinking. Burglary, theft, robbery, mugging helpless people is somehow justified and tolerated in order to protect the rights of suspects and to give offenders a second chance. Nothing wrong with that, but *one* second chance is all they get! We know through trial and error that a thug with a rap sheet of five, ten, twenty, fifty, sometimes over one hundred offenses, is not going to change his or her ways as long as the system is not changed.

The laws should be crystal clear, this offense equals this penalty. No exceptions! If you are old enough to plan and execute the crime, you are old enough to face and pay the penalty. Little kids understand that perfectly when their parents enforce the rules. The penalties must be clear and severe. There will be some hapless criminals sacrificed to establish that the law means what it says. They asked for it, they get it, that's fair. For capital crimes there should be *no* second chance. Rapists, murders and all capital offenders deserve the maximum penalty the law allows. No blaming their parents or some lame excuse of abuse in their childhood. After age twelve you know right from wrong enough to know that if you do the crime you do the time. No phony insanity defense or excuses such as being under the influence of drugs or alcohol at the time of the event. That is the price you pay when you take the chance to drink the alcohol or take the drugs.

There needs to be substantial penalties for drug users and severe penalties for drug dealers at all levels. But, as always, the people involved blame someone or something else. The users blame the dealers and the system, using every excuse they can come up with: they are stressed, confused, depressed, etc.,etc.. The dealers blame the users and the system and the cartels, the cartels and governments blame each other, etc., etc.. Personal responsibility is not a part of the equation. If you eliminate the market by eliminating the users, the dealer is out of business. If you eliminate both, one at a time if necessary, you eventually run out of people involved in drugs.

Case in point. China had an equally or possibly more advanced drug problem with opium and heroin than the USA has with it's current population's drugs of choice until the Communists came into power in the middle of the twentieth century. They eliminated the users and dealers and producers by eliminating them one at a time when necessary, by execution when necessary. A television documentary showed an actual case of an adult man caught dealing drugs in a part of China so remote that it was a day long trip by horseback to the nearest village. The man was paraded through his village and forced to carry a large cross on his back which identified him and his crime. He was then taken by motorcycle to a pre dug hole the exact dimensions of his size to receive his body whereupon he was stood in front of the hole and killed with a bullet to the head. His body fell into the hole and was left for his family to deal with the disposal. The family was presented with a bill from the government for the equivalent of seven cents to cover the cost of the bullet. That kind of action begets attention! The next thug contemplating making a drug sale just might consider a change of career and lifestyle.

Severe?

Yes!

Effective?

100%.

#4

DEMAND RESPONSIBILITY AND ACCOUNTABILITY

The United States and the world needs to return to common sense responsibility and accountability. Why should an employer be forced by federal law to hire someone to fill a job or position if the person is somebody he or she would prefer not to associate with? Why should a landlord be required to rent his property to a tenant when he knows the arrangement is doomed to failure? When a prospective employee or tenant shows up looking like something out of a freak show why should he or she expect and demand the same consideration as a clean cut and appropriately dressed applicant? The reason is because if he or she has reasonably comparable credentials *it is the law!*

Take a look at city, county, state and federal employees doing work not described as "white collar"jobs. Scraggly beards, long unkempt hair, head rags, clothing that looks like it's been slept in is all too common. Also very common among this bunch is the laid back attitude that "I will do just enough to meet the job description and requirements and nothing more." Add to that the surly attitude of many of these people. They apparently do not understand that they are employed by and working for John Q. Public. The smug look on the faces of those with vested rights is disturbing. Together with their white collar counterparts they form a workforce that in too many cases could not compete and survive in the business world.

Consider a comparison of a small business owner and one of these government employees. It is almost universal that a guy or gal who owns and operates his or her own business is working as hard and fast and smart as they possibly can. You can reasonably expect to be greeted with a pleasant greeting and a smile. They operate under the basic concept that "the customer is always right." Not so with the typical oh-so-official white collar bureaucrat or the four guys leaning on shovels watching the fifth guy dig a hole.

You have seen them. I personally watched a middle aged man with severe arthritis in his hands leisurely brush his hair, get a cup of coffee, brush his hair some more then refresh his coffee in a Department Of Transportation office at opening time in the morning while a dozen or so customers cooled their heels. It was about forty five minutes before he opened his window and snarled at the first customer, me! Meanwhile the other window persons waited on other customers in a laid back fashion as if time was of no importance. Evidently time is not important to them probably because they make the same amount of money whether they hustle a little or just grind out their shift. They work for a monopoly that does not have to compete. The guy with the severe arthritis could not possibly preform any demanding physical work, you would think that he might appreciate the job he has and make an effort as a token of appreciation.

Frequently at break time bureaucrats happily close the window in your face and mosey off to wherever they go. People in small businesses routinely miss their coffee breaks and lunches and dinners to take care of business and customers. What a contrast! Maybe these bureaucrats need to spend a few days in the orange orchards or the tomato fields!

The county employees where I live recently received an across the board ten percent pay raise! It is difficult to believe that everyone of those employees was performing their work at the highest obtainable level! Ten percent is a huge pay raise, it was explained that it was necessary in order to compete with other counties in our part of the country. It is extremely hard for me to believe after having been told by one of our outstanding county employees in effect to "tell someone who cares" when I complained, politely I might add, about being put on hold for about twenty minutes before she answered my call.

The obvious solution to this problem is to make pay relative to performance in real terms, the same with teachers at all levels. When there is little or no incentive to do better or work harder you can expect these kinds of performances and results. (Coincidently I was shopping in a big name grocery store recently, mostly because the price was right on some featured items. The employees there resembled a bunch of old time carnival workers more than the modern day grocery store employees I expected to see with their goatees, beards, spiked hair, tattoos and poorly chosen clothing. There was a $7.00 overcharge on my receipt, it took two clowns and one incompetent ringmaster to straighten it out. I will vote with my dollars and avoid that store whenever possible!) The degeneration seems to be everywhere, with no end in sight.

An employer should have the freedom of choice to hire whomever he or she chooses. A landlord should have the same latitude on choosing a tenant. The spirit of the laws governing these equal rights under the law protections had good intent, no doubt. The practical application is too often a failure and a legal nightmare. When your intuition and your gut tells you that a prospective worker or renter is not the right person for the situation you should be able to say no and be reasonably accountable to no one for your decision. Of course there will be those who abuse any system. As it is now the more frequent abusers are the people who instantly scream *discrimination* when they are rejected or don't like what they hear about rules, regulations, job requirements, etc.. etc..

Let's say for illustration purposes that you own a beach house in Malibu, California. You will be away for a year on a project and think it would be good economically to rent your home during your absence. You have two prospects who meet you at the property separately.

The first prospect is a businessman with a wife and two children who will live at the house on a full time basis while they have a new home built. The family meets your expectations in regard to appearance and manners and assure you that they can qualify with a credit check and financial requirements. You notice that their car is clean and appears to be well taken care of. The kids show respect as they go through the place checking it out and deciding who gets which room. Your overall impression of the family is good. You ask them to fill out an application and inform them that you will check their credit.

You arrive at the property at the appointed time to meet the next prospect. You wait fifteen minutes during which time there is no call on your cell phone from the person you are there to meet. After a few more minutes you are about to leave when the man arrives with three homeboys in a very expensive sports car. Loud rap music booms from the stereo, the prospect greets you, three other young men take their time extracting themselves from the car and make no effort to acknowledge you or be sociable. You knew from your initial conversation that the prospect was a black entertainer, you are not prejudiced, but you did not expect to see body piercings, massive tattoos, a disrespectful attitude, and three hangers on. (I didn't say one thing about Dennis Rodman!) You assume from what you see and hear that he can meet the credit check and financial requirements, he tells you that he has another home back east and that he will only be in this house when he is in California on business or an occasional vacation. As you show them the house you observe the three friends taking mental possession, carelessly slamming doors, showing indifference and disrespect for you and your property.

What are you going to do? The prospective renter knows that it is available now and tells you he will take it. You take the only evasive action you can, you tell him you are accepting formal applications and will do a credit check. The credit check is your last hope to disqualify this prospect, it is used routinely by rental professionals as a last resort when other requirements pass the test. You are very aware that you are wide open for a discrimination suit if you choose applicant number one, if this man meets the criteria, and that this guy just might do it if your intuition is correct. On the other hand you know that you have a responsibility to your neighbors and that you will be hearing from them if there is loud music and wild parties. You also have deep concerns about what condition your home will be in when the renter moves out.

Instead or you being the owner of a Malibu beach house let's say you own a duplex. You live in one unit and count on the rental income to help pay the mortgage. It is not in the best neighborhood in small town America, but it suits your needs. There are no responses to your rental ad in the local paper for a few days so you are getting a little nervous. Then out of the blue you get a call, a man and his girlfriend want to look at the duplex. You set an appointment and meet them there on time.

Your worst fears are realized as the car drives up. It is beat up, filthy, the windows are greased with fingerprints and a big friendly dog hangs out one side window wagging his tail at you. The music is rockin! The guy steps out, he has long dirty hair, tattoos, body piercings featuring spikes in his lips, multiple rings in his eyebrows, and a ring in his tongue . His clothes are the "grunge look," he wears his baseball cap backwards. His name is Jason, he introduces you to his "old lady" Megan and their kid Katlin. The mother needs a shampoo and a shower, the baby a diaper change and a bath. She's obviously quite pregnant again, she hangs Katlin on her hip and her eyes don't look up to meet yours. You can't end the interview at this point so you go through the motions. As Megan enters the living room she trips on her three inch high footwear, Katlin's juice bottle adds some color to your carpet. Jason tells you that he does drywall work for a local company and that he has been employed there for five years, he has pretty good credit and he has money for first, last and a cleaning deposit. He says it's just what they have been looking for, she nods in agreement, and he says "We'll take it!"

What in the hell are you going to do? This guy knows the unit is available or you wouldn't be there. He evidently could qualify based on what he has told you and he probably knows the ropes regarding the rental game. You need the income, but do you need it that bad? No way!You would be discriminating if you indicated or told them you do not like what you see. These people are not exactly what you had in mind to be your duplex-next-door-neighbors. Your last line of defense is the good old application and credit check double shuffle routine. The fact that you consider it to be a nightmare in the making and a train wreck in the end cannot be a consideration. What's wrong with this picture?

There are many things wrong with this picture, and the one presented by Malibu renter number two. Number one is that we all need to be held personally responsible for our actions. If you choose to act, dress, and present yourself in ways that you know are personally offensive to other people you need to be prepared to pay the price. It is ludicrous to expect other people to accommodate your deviant behavior, and for them to be bound by outlandish laws to do things they do not want to do.

What can be done about it? If there is a majority of people left in this country, and I question whether there is, who have their heads on straight, we will have to organize and revolt against these ridiculous rules and laws and demand a return to sensibility and personal responsibility. The entertainment industry, and Hollywood in particular, who sets the pace for vulgarity, indecency and disrespect must be reined in. It does not require an uprising in the streets at this point, rather a long slow climb up the road we just rolled down. Talk to your family, your neighbors and friends, find out what can be done and what you can do, if you think there needs to be a change. You will have an opportunity the next time there is an election at any level if you get out there and make your voice heard. You can get involved in a new effort that will be discussed next.

There is always a long shot possibility that a strong leader will arise from among the ranks who, with the backing of a like minded majority, will demand and lead repeal of these ridiculous laws, inspire a change of attitudes, and a return to civility. I think George W. Bush was the right man for the job at the time he was elected if the country had been in a state of mind to assign the task to him and back him up.

Remember that he was elected before the attacks of 9/11/2001, when "touchy-feely" attitudes were at their peak.

There was absolutely no chance of a change of direction at that moment in time. As an example, he was heavily criticized for announcing that Osama bin Ladin was, in the vernacular if the Old West, "WANTED DEAD OR ALIVE!" It was too harsh for politically correct ears! It is ironic that it is now acceptable to report the death of terrorists in very graphic terms, even to televise pictures of Saddam Hussein's dead sons and recently Abu Musab al Zarqawi displayed dead for all the world to see. Maybe things are changing, reality coming into play. Bush's popularity has taken a beating in the polls because people want the war to end quickly like it does on TV, before the end of the hour, or within a miniseries at the max. That's just not how the real world works. Fortunately George W. does not make decisions based on his rating in the polls. He has the internal courage, dedication and common sense to do what is best for America. Now would be a great time for people to quit dreaming and criticizing and get behind a good leader while we are fortunate enough to have one.

In the absence of such a leader appearing, there is an opportunity at hand to do something proactive, something that you can do, something that could perhaps *really* get some results and *make a difference.*

I propose that an organization be formed as quickly as possible to stand up for the rights and principals that this country was founded upon, some of which have been discussed herein. I would suggest that it be called SANE AMERICANS FOR AMERICA until and unless someone comes up with a better name. SAFA, for short, would be the opposite of the ultra liberal ACLU. This is not to say that the ACLU has not done some good things throughout it's history, it has. The purpose and intent of SAFA would be to recruit people who believe in these ideals to support and defend against challenges to what we believe in, the same way that the ACLU is organized and funded to promote what they believe in. As it is, at this point in time, individuals, businesses and organizations who confront or are confronted with a contentious issue many times must go it alone against the powerful and well funded ACLU. The proposed SAFA would come to their aid in a well funded and organized way to stand with them, particularly in legal matters, while defending the issue in contention from a conservative viewpoint at the same time. I am certainly not making a sales pitch for myself here. I am not qualified nor interested in running such an organization, but I will gladly do anything reasonable and within my abilities to help organize and get such an organization off of the ground.

In addition to the above mentioned goals, SAFA could become the standard bearer for what is simple common sense and what is right. We have laws on the books for just about everything, SAFA would put some pressure on those responsible to enforce these laws. We have rules regarding immigration which have been sadly neglected, SAFA could demand enforcing the laws we have and have a voice in creating new laws to deal with the immigration issue as it develops. SAFA could attempt to help people understand the value of our existing laws and the value received in respecting these laws. As it is now, the predominate mind set in America is not to operate within the law, but to see what you can get away with too much of the time. People in general, and young people in particular, routinely break the law when driving by speeding, tailgating, passing in the turn lane and cutting in front of others dangerously close, as an example. They seem to take pride in their aggressive actions instead of having the satisfaction of having done what is courteous and correct and legal. These same type of people use threating language, gestures, and body language to intimidate people who are obeying the law and doing what is courteous, correct and legal. They attempt to twist the facts to make you feel as if you are the offender for obeying the laws. They park in disabled only spaces for their own convenience, although they are not disabled, and do not display disabled license plates or tags. They violate common sense and decency when they blast others with extremely loud music and/or loud exhaust systems, thereby invading the peace and quiet that we should expect to be protected. Harley Davidson riders are among the worst, and there are going to be more and more of them as the current fad continues. At what point did the rights to peace and quiet and the pursuit of happiness become a distant second to a minority who like to blast our senses with their loud engines and/or earth shaking music? For the record, I have ridden motorcycles and quad runners for more that thirty five years. I see no correlation between the enjoyment of riding and the necessity of invading someone else's right to peace and quiet by blasting their senses with excessive and unnecessary noise. Quite often one rider's macho feeling of power and the satisfaction the noise brings to him or her invades the peace and quiet of many other people. Ditto with excessively loud power boats, cars and trucks. Why are the laws on the books regarding loud exhausts and loud music rarely enforced? A worthwhile project for the proposed SAFA?

It is common to see vehicles with city, county, state and federal government emblems speeding; including police, sheriff, and highway patrol cars, when there is obviously no emergency. Private business vehicles, public utility vehicles, all sorts of private cars and trucks breaking the speed laws, and those who should be protecting public safety by enforcing the laws among them. There appears to be a generation or two of young law enforcement officers who have grown up in a time and place where they did not have the experience nor see the results of others respecting the laws and plain common sense. It appears that they somehow expect people to speed, tailgate, cut in front of other vehicles, break a variety of laws, and they do nothing unless the violation is extreme. These are a few examples of matters that the SAFA could address and begin to bring some pressure to bear to make a change. The organization could be a shining light for those who have had no one or nothing to look up to begin to understand that we have laws for legitimate reasons, and that there is real value in it for them to respect the law and others, and receive the benefits in return.

There is also another possibility that this wonderful country could collapse from rot on the inside like many other counties who's people devoted themselves to debauchery and self indulgence such as Greece, The Roman Empire, France, etc.,etc..

I just heard another rumble, rather a shaking of the earth by giant footsteps, caused by a giant dragon called China who has enough population and financial clout to smash us like a bug on a windshield with their population of 1,300,000,000 compared to our measly soon to be 300,000,000 or so if it so desired. As I said before, empires can collapse from within, a recent example being the Soviet Union largely for economic reasons. Imagine the clout of a nation with the population and financial power of China to give a little shove at the appropriate moment and you do not have to be a genius to imagine the result. China has the equivalent of something on the order of $675,000,000,000 in savings accounts at this writing, the USA has a negative account balance, is a net borrower, and China is loaning us a lot of the money, buying our debt. So is Japan. China is also on a buying binge, they are buying up commodities and producers of commodities in general and oil companies in particular. They have a huge amount of cash with which to do it. We're talking about a sleeping giant with superior brain power in the pipeline, huge cash reserves, and about a billion and one third people! Just imagine what they could do in a few short years if more aggressive military minds were to take over! That may not be necessary, China could reduce us to a second rate power, or worse, with her financial might alone under certain conditions. This does not mean that The United States would fall off of the face of the earth, it simply means that we would no longer be what we are now. What that would be is anyone's guess! And don't overlook a population of nearly 1,000,000,00 and the financial capacity of India for the same reasons!

So here we are at a crossroads. Do we begin to see and try to understand the problems, or do we just look the other way and try to focus on the bright side? Do we do what we can to attempt to educate and encourage people to step up to the plate and do their part? To take responsibility, to be accountable, to realize some sense of satisfaction and self esteem from their efforts. To curb criminal activity and general disobedience. Do we give new generations of little kids and young adults a fighting chance by correcting our mistakes of the past?

The giant oak tree is now totally infested with disrespect, discontent, and the drug scourge to the extent that now even the acorns are passing along the drugs in their system to the next new trees. We have generations of people who were born addicted to drugs while in their mothers womb, or mentally affected by the drugs the mothers took while pregnant, or drugs the father and/or mother took before the children were conceived. This can't continue if America is to remain strong and proud. Like America, the mighty oak tree is rotting on the inside. Can either continue to weather the storm, even to stand?

Could another strong blow or two knock them down? How many nine elevens and Katrinas can we stand? What if we are hit with a dirty bomb or two in the agricultural centers of our food supply?

Katrina could be a blessing in disguise if we are smart enough to read the signs. What do you think?

CHAPTER SEVEN

A POSITIVE AND REALISTIC APPROACH TO RESOLVING THE RACE ISSUE IN AMERICA

What has long been called a *race* issue in The United States Of America is in fact a *nationality and cultural* issue. People of all nationalities, races, colors, religions and beliefs have risen to positions of power and high office, especially in the last five decades. From school teachers to bureaucrats to business people to TV newscasters to journalists to law enforcement officials to politicians at high levels, people of all nationalities, races and creeds have succeeded and are represented. Their nationality or race may have hindered them or it may have helped them, that is part of any equation. But it did not stop them. After all *John F Kennedy* was an Irish Catholic, almost forgotten now, but a huge obstacle to him in his day!

Let's get it straight once and for all. Every person born in the United States is born with *equal* rights, at birth there is absolutely no nationality or race issue regarding equal rights. Your nationality is *American.* It is guaranteed by the constitution of the United Stated

Of America. The culture they grow up in and the decisions they make will determine whether they benefit from understanding this inalienable right, or choose to ignore it and pass their ignorance and failures off as problems beyond their control because of their race. It is clearly a *cultural* issue because it is their *culture* and their decisions that set them apart, not their *race*. Why do we let a *cultural* issue masquerade as a *race* issue? You are judged by what you do rather than what you are.

There certainly was a time when America was a racist country. Starting the day that the first European immigrants set foot on what was to be called America there was a confrontation in the works between the settlers and the natives called Indians. Through misunderstanding, mistrust, greed, broken promises and savage brutality on both sides, the struggle to control the continent and it's riches, although actually based on culture and politics, became a race war, the "white man" versus the native Indian people, the "red man." Believe it or not, later on there were black soldiers helping to overwhelm the "red man." Unfair, unjust and devastating to the people who occupied the land in the first place, the Indian tribes and people were relocated, eradicated and hammered into submission. A terrible chapter in American history.

Then came immigrants from most places on the face of the globe, different waves at different times for different reasons, not necessarily in the following order. Mexican people were in the southwestern part of the continent long before explorers from the east ventured west, they continued to come and continue to come to this day. Their culture is forever ingrained in America, and in the southwest in particular. The struggle for control of the land could be called a race war, "brown" people versus "white people," when in fact it was, and is, a political and *cultur*al war. There was plenty of friction between the Mexicans and the settlers, including a major conflict called the Mexican American War. The Mexican people have been given derogatory names such as "Wet Backs," "Beaners" etc.,etc.. The Germans came bringing with them their culture and ways that were different from the early Europeans who preceded them, primarily the English. These differences caused friction and confrontations over time. They were called " krauts" as well as other derogatory names. Italians came to the land of opportunity and, because of their culture and ways, were not welcomed with open arms, but allowed because many could and would do hard manual labor. They were called WOPS which was derived from the phrase "With Out Papers." Certainly not a nice label to put on an entire nationality of people. The Scandinavian people came in masses and settled throughout the country as it was at the time. In the nineteenth century they were in the majority of people who settled the upper mid west and northern great plains, which nobody wanted up to that time except Indian people and the railroads. They were looked down upon by some Easterners, who by that time thought themselves to be above the class of the new arrivals. They were called "Hard Headed Swedes," the Norwegians were called "Swedes with their brains knocked out," and visa versa. Polish people were known as "Poles" and "Pollocks." Czechoslovakian people as "Checks," Slavic people as "Slavs," Russians as "Ruskies," etc.,etc.. The Irish were particularly looked down upon because they were extremely poor and because of their rough and rowdy ways and their tendency to fight at the drop of a hat. They acquired the moniker of "Micks" and "Paddys" and other not complimentary names. The words are not necessarily offensive words, but the inferences are. These different nationalities grouped together in the cities and lived in a culture reminiscent of their homeland, naturally. The struggles were not *race* issues, these people were predominately white, they were *cultural* issues.

These peoples were obviously very different as defined by their culture, but they had one thing in common. They were, including the Latinos who were not known as "brown" people, called "white people." Over time they integrated into the greater American society in different ways and to different levels, and they became Americans. They still lived in culturally flavored communities, slowly but surely moving out and into the mainstream. They did not particularly want or need to be known as Mexican Americans, German Americans, Italian Americans, Swedish Americans, Norwegian Americans, Polish Americans, Czechoslovakian Americans, Slavic Americans, Russian Americans, or Irish Americans. They were by and large proud and happy to be just Americans. It is high time for black people to stop demanding to be known as African Americans or any other special designation. Be happy to know that if you were born here or have become naturalized you are accepted as just plain Americans, like all the rest of us, and do nothing to demean the name. Be proud of it, protect it and defend it.

The Chinese immigrants had a tough row to hoe because they were not generally included as whites. They were called "Chinks" and "Coolies" and a host of other defamatory names, but they too wanted to become Americans and most worked hard at doing so. They also lived in cultural enclaves known as China Towns, but went about their business and integrated at their particular speed and in their own way. They do not demand to be known as "Chinese Americans" or "Oriental Americans."

Most of the "white people", Oriental peoples, and the Mexican people did have, and do have, one thing in common; they came here and continue to come here to try to improve the quality of their lives of their own choice, with a few notable exceptions. Indentured workers, sex slaves, political and religious refugees etc.,etc., are examples of people who may have preferred to remain in their native land but were forced to leave and wound up in America.

The black people forcibly brought from Africa to America as slaves were a totally different story. They did not come here of their own free will to try to improve their quality of life. On the other hand they were brought to the land of opportunity, which in time would benefit their descendants when those descendants took advantage of the opportunities. Most other immigrants gave up their homeland, their families, their money, and some their lives attempting to come here. *Do not overlook this fact*! Todays black American people should remember that the terrible condition of their ancestors is the price that was paid for their birthright as free Americans. We of other national origins should also remember that our ancestors also paid a very high price for the rights that we enjoy today. We all need to learn and understand that it was easy for no one, and that it is futile to blame the actions of any of our ancestors for the conditions we find ourselves in today. That time has long since past, we are now responsible for our own actions and well being.

It is also a fact that if you truly hate America you are free to go to the land of your ancestors or any other country of your choosing that will accept you. No one is forcing you to stay in this country, unless of course you are incarcerated, regardless of race, religion, creed or nationality. When you denounce, unfairly criticize and attack America and attempt to tear it down you had better realize that you are are also destroying the house that you live in, so to speak. Either get involved and contribute something to make it better or move to where life would be better for you. Straighten up and fly right or move on, don't be a burden to others. Stop repeatedly biting the hand that feeds you. To quote *John F. Kennedy*,"Ask not what your country can do for you, ask what you can do for your country."

The practice of slavery is, however, probably the saddest, most brutal, disturbing, distasteful and unnecessary chapter in American history. It has been proved unnecessary because this country has successfully moved forward after slavery was abolished some one hundred and forty six years ago. The freed black people have overcome seemingly insurmountable obstacles and have made giant strides moving forward as well. And therein lies the key to a possible end of the stigma of the race problem; we have proved that we can survive without each other, and we have proved that we can benefit from working with each other. After one hundred and forty six years it is time to bury the hatchet and make the best of the situation as it is. Black people of America, once and for all refrain from playing the race card. Do not degrade your stature by demanding to be addressed as anything other than Americans like the rest of us.

I have never researched, read , heard or been told where the "N" word came from. It is a moot point because it is so ingrained and controversial in our language that it's origin is of little consequence. Because much of the slave trade was conducted in or through Nigeria it is possible and logical to assume that the "N" word was given as a name to the people taken from or through there, much the same as Swedish people were called Swedes, Czechoslovakians called Checks, Polish people called Poles, etc.,etc., although they may have originally come from or been a part of another country at one time. While the Mexicans, Europeans, and Orientals and the rest were, and no doubt are, offended by the nicknames given to them, there was and is the stigma of slavery, and all of it's negative inferences, in the use the "N" word to identify the African people, regardless of where they came from. It is certainly justifiable and understandable why they resent being thrown together in one all inclusive group identified by that name. But black people of America understand that you are now accepted as *Americans,* no additional description is necessary. What you do with this wonderful opportunity is based on your *culture and your actions, not your race.*

What's in a name? What makes one name acceptable to a group of people, and another name offensive and disrespectful. Suppose for conversation sake that the word *beautiful* meant that you were ugly. No one would want to be told that they are beautiful. Conversely let's suppose that *repulsive* meant that you were attractive and desirable when somebody complementing you told you that you are repulsive. A name assigned to a condition, example good or bad, or perception, example beautiful or ugly, or a people designates what that word means to us when we hear it. We automatically make a decision on condition, perception or people when we hear a certain word. Until recently the use of the "N" word immediately conjured up the image of black people, too often *all* black people, with no distinction between a person of high character and a thug robbing a liquor store. The actions of the latter denigrates the entire race and contributes to the negative perception of the word. The point here is *what* is the perception of the person hearing the word? In this case does the speaker mean all black people, or is it a derogatory inference to some black people, or is he or she a late night black comedian using the word to give a friendly jab to another black "sister"or "brother?" The former is offensive, the later acceptable under the circumstances. The perception is the key.

At the time that slavery was abolished the "N" word in The United States, as they were at that time, meant a person of African origin whether born here or there. It also meant all of the things that related to the perception of those people at that time, examples being slave or ex-slave, ignorant, illiterate, inferior, lazy, all of the other negative connotations that the word meant at that time and place. That was a hundred and forty six years ago. Except for the slave inference of course, it loosely means those same things to a segment of American black people today, those who denigrate the race through their words and actions.

There is a distinction today between the black people who integrate into the American system and way of life, and those who do not. No one can play the race card legitimately when you look at the success of Colin Powell or Condolezza Rice or any number of African Americans who have climbed the ladder of success overcoming whatever obstacles they encountered along the way, the same as any other nationality has to do. The reason I used these two people as examples is that I believe that Colon Powell could have been a real contender in a contest to be President of The United States, if he had chose to do so, and Condaleezza Rice is in a like position at the present time. Conversely it is the segment of black people who cling to the well established life style of take all you can get from the government, don't bother with getting an education or self improvement, blame all of your problems on the government and white people, expect them in turn to solve all of your problems, meanwhile you give nothing back, who choose to complain about a race problem and play the race card in almost every contentious situation. It is a *cultural* problem, quite obviously not a *race* problem.

Realizing that the heart of the problem is a *cultural* problem not a *race* problem provides a fresh new positive approach to finding a solution suitable to all parties involved. Where and how to begin?

The answer is the same as it is for the civil disorder, disrespect for everything issue and the drug problem. *Dig sown to bedrock..* To repeat, we must get the very young children off on the right foot and guide them through their high school education and their required year of service to the country with an unyielding hand. This will break the cycle of repeating the same mistakes that has created these enormous social problems. There is no issue of race in this approach, it is to be applied evenly regardless of nationality, race, religion, belief, or station in life. And again we must put aside for the moment those who cannot and will not respond to efforts made to attempt to help them turn their lives around until the dig *down to bedrock* programs are firmly in place and operating.

Rule number one when it's time to deal with the incorrigibles is that *every man woman and child is responsible for their own conduct and well being and will be held accountable.* Not the government, not their parents, not the Social Services or the churches, not me. These people will have choices to make, either get into the program and make the best of it or pay the price for non compliance. *Workfare, not welfare* will be the buzz word. Those who are actually physically or mentally disabled and the elderly will be adequately provided for, and subject to accountable certification. For those who accept the challenge and the appropriate program, the amount of money paid in the past as welfare will now be paid for work performed, with a suggested time limit of six months to acquire some skills and integrate into the work force. After that they will need to compete in the open marketplace like everyone else. Failure to accept and begin, or failure to succeed will bear the obvious consequences. There is one final option to be discussed a bit later, leave the country.

There will be no *second chance programs.* For those who choose to do nothing or make a feeble attempt and fail, they will accept the consequences of their actions. They make a choice, the result has to be expected, and therefore it is their suitable solution as a result of their decisions.

Obviously this leaves open the question of what will happen to those who refuse to participate, or try and fail but refuse to leave the country. Will they not turn to, or return to, crime to support themselves? The answer is without a doubt, yes they will. What is the solution to this threatening and unacceptable problem?

The answer is that the current American generations and all levels of government and law enforcement must return to reality to deal with the problems of mugging, holdups, burglary, robbery, home invasions, smash and grab and all other forms of theft of property, and all capital crimes. The "touchy-feely" approach has not worked, is not working and will not work. The theory that almost any person who has gone astray can be turned around with soft sentences, counseling, community service etc.,etc., must be scrapped and the principles that were applied in harder times reinstated. A people living in fear and terror in their own homes who fear leaving their homes and walking or driving on the streets do not fit the definition of a *free* people.

During a catastrophe in the early twentieth century in San Francisco the civil authorities lost control of the city and looting was running rampant. A tough old military officer was put in charge to get things under control and he stopped the looting in *one hour* after giving orders to his troops. His order? *Shoot to kill*! It doesn't sound like

America today, it doesn't sound nice, and it is not nice! That is beside the point, that is what it took to stop the problem! That is what it will take to stop the problems in this country today! When law enforcement could not control the criminal behavior in New Orleans after the Katrina hurricane and flooding the National Guard quickly brought the situation under not complete but better control with the *shoot to kill* doctrine.

When an officer of the law orders a person to *stop* or *halt* that command should be followed instantly and it should mean exactly what it says. It should not mean that a person can run, resist, fight or try to escape if the offender is driving a car or on foot. The officer should be authorized by virtue of his badge to shoot to kill when the order is not obeyed. Why put innocent people and the officer himself or herself in harms way and in life threatening situations because we don't have the guts to stop the suspect or offender in his tracks when he refuses to obey an order. How many times do we have to see officers of the law in a physical fight for his or her life, or a gun fight because the person ordered to surrender knows that the officer's hands are tied regarding the amount of physical force he or she is allowed to use to subdue the person he or she is trying to stop? Think of all of the innocent people who's injuries and lives could be saved in the future if those wild car chases we see on TV were largely a thing of the past because the bad guys were made to understand that there is absolute zero tolerance for noncompliance when a stop order is given. They need to understand that the next thing that is going to happen if they don't obey an order is that they are going to be shot, probably killed! The same goes for muggers, robbers, looters and the rest who refuse to obey commands. Granted there will be mistakes made, but the biggest mistake will be to do nothing and let the innocent suffer and die to protect the suspects and offenders. A great side benefit would be that it would not take six or eight officers and a K-9 unit to handle the arrest of one person and other run-of-the- mill situations as it does too often today. One officer with the authority to use all force necessary, and a backup as needed, would be sufficient. The rest of the officers could be out protecting someone else, doing their job, subduing another law breaker. Maybe we would not need so many police officers.

When I was a youngster in Montana there was a no-nonsense Montana Highway Patrolman named Eugene "Gene" Mora. (I hope the spelling is correct.) Everybody that lived in that part of the country knew that when he turned his red spotlight on you, you had better pull over. He didn't call for backup. He would stop you, bring you in if necessary one way or the other, your choice. Always fair and respected, he had very few problems as far as I ever knew. I never once heard of a complaint against him. It has been done, it could be done again. This is an excellent example of how to end the circus atmosphere in law enforcement today as exemplified by "Cops" and other such TV productions. Hollywood is not going to like this!

And what a sad state of affairs it is when today a person suspected of a crime has to be referred to as a "person of interest" instead of a suspect! Another travesty is that it is common to hear it said on TV that a suspect is *innocent until proven guilty.* Isn't the letter of the law that a person is *presumed* innocent until proven guilty? A bank robber caught in the act and stopped by a policeman *is* guilty. The documentation of his actions in a court of law *proves* him guilty. And when an officer of the law calls the "person of interest" a *"gentleman"* it raises the hair on the back of my neck! The combined words, *gentle* and *man,* are insulted when a murderer or rapist or any other criminal is called a "gentleman." The same goes for females who are criminals, they certainly are not *ladies.* Come on people, get your use of the English language straight!

It was sickening to watch on television the looters in New Orleans rampaging through the city not only looting, but smashing, grabbing, destroying, taking things they did not need to survive. Smashing expensive store fronts to get at the merchandise inside. Stolen grocery carts often filled to the top with more items than the thief needed to survive for a few days, or for a family to survive until things returned to normal. People loaded with boxes of new shoes that you know were far beyond the realm of actual need. Thieves boldly rolling and carrying luxury items down the flooded streets, TVs, stereos, refrigerators, furniture, you name it. Many looked brazenly into the cameras as if to say "what are you gonna do about it?" There was much debate on the news shows and elsewhere about whether it was acceptable to steal what you need to survive as compared to grabbing excessive or luxury items that you do not need to survive. *That is the world's biggest slippery slope*! Who is to decide when enough is enough? The answer is straight forward and simple, no one has the right to steal *any* property to fill *any* need that person might have! Period! In dire need it is understandable if someone uses or takes possession of property that belongs to others when the opportunity to ask permission is not possible. With that goes the responsibility to respect that property, take care of it and return it or replace it when possible. There are extenuating circumstances in some cases, and exceptions to every rule, but that should be the rule.

Would it not have been much better for people in dire need of food, water, medicine and other staples of life in New Orleans to have organized themselves in a responsible manner and have doled out what there was in a sensible orderly fashion. There was no need to destroy a Wal-Mart store. Wal-Mart is among the worlds best corporations when it comes to helping people in need. The waste and destruction of those and so many other stores was a testament to the attitude of civil disobedience running rampant throughout the country today. It can incorrectly be called a *race* problem when it is in fact a *cultural* problem.

Both black and "white"people were involved in the crimes, the looting, the violence and disregard for the law. Therefore it is not simply a race problem. It is a cultural problem dating back for many generations, but brought to the current level beginning with the drug culture and the warehousing of people under the umbrella of The Great Society. Who was it great for? Not the people who received it, look at what it has done to them. Not for the taxpayers who payed for it, look at the result and how their money was wasted. Not for the government, look at the administrative nightmare and bureaucracy it has created with no end in sight.

There is however difference between races in regard to attitude and responsibility that can be documented. According to the news reports the estimated ratio of people living in the projects and the areas of New Orleans that did not evacuate was somewhere in the area of sixty seven percent black, thirty three percent white, give or take a few points. It would therefore be logical to assume that for every three white people looting and rampaging there would be seven black people doing the same things. There is no way to know if or not that assumption held true. What was clearly evident from what was shown on TV was that there was a difference in the attitude of the looters. There was a defiance and a viciousness far above and beyond the realm of necessity for food, water and clothing displayed by the blacks as they looted, smashed, grabbed and destroyed other people's property that was not evident in the attitude and actions of the white people doing the same things. The hatred for authority at all levels, and of government in particular, that came through the TV screen was a clear picture of the mentality of the black people living in the areas shown and in the projects of New Orleans today. It is in fact a cultural problem. It is symbolic of the cultural problem throughout the United States today. What has caused this deep rooted problem?

The problem undoubtedly goes back as far as the history of slavery in America. It is logical to assume that the enslaved people more than resented being captured and forced into slavery, and all of the sub human treatment they endured as such, they surely hated their circumstances and the people who imposed slavery upon them. As the generations succeeded one another there was an attitude of acceptance and civility that evidently developed over the years which allowed the slave owners, their families, slave bosses and the enslaved people to live in a workable coexistence, if not an entirely peaceful one. As history tells the story that is a broad picture of the situation up to the time of the Civil War. When emancipated, many black people and their families stayed on with their former owners for their own reasons, some because they felt comfortable and thought it was best for them, many because they had no experience or idea of how to do anything else. Where were they to go? What would they do?

Eventually the freed black people integrated at their pace into the mainstream of America, some learned skills, some became educated, most worked at improving their station in life. They gravitated from the plantations and farms to the cities where there was work to be had. Naturally in the cities they gathered with their own kind of people in neighborhoods, in many cases becoming the majority of the people in the city. Harlem is a good example of a city with a culture and it's own identity as a city made up of primarily black people.

Form the days following the Civil War up to the time of the Civil Rights Movements of the 1960s the definition of black people as "colored people, or "people of color" seemed to be acceptable as a way to describe and identify black people. With the advent of the "Black Power Movement" and other such activist activities those terms were deemed to be dated, identifying an old outdated image of a subdued, passive black people. The new acceptable term was "black people," "people of African heritage," or the most widely accepted "African Americans." The demand for black people to have an equal place in American society, educational opportunities, work and business opportunities, was absolutely correct and justifiable.

Like almost any other political situation or upheaval, there were and are those who take advantage of an opportunity and make the most of it. Unfortunately there is always an element that takes advantage the other way, the negative way. Take and give nothing back. To those I say "Enough already! Such a deal I've got for you!" I propose a new government program. Black, white, or any other people that continue to bite the hand that feeds you listen up! Your plight is partly the fault of the United States government for teaching you to be dependent on someone else besides yourself. If you have not used this as a safety net and made something of yourself or become self reliant, you are therefore also at fault. So here's the deal. Get your personal house in order because you will be given a dated notice after which you will have a specific number of Social Security or other welfare payments coming, I suggest six, no more. The money that would have continued to come as welfare, or *workfare* if you choose that program and fail, will now be used to buy you a one way airplane ticket to any country of your choice that will accept you. Any of your immediate family who receives Social Security payments will also receive a ticket, if they so choose. Refusal to accept this or one of the programs to learn to work within the suggested six month maximum period will automatically mean immediate cancellation of your Social Security or other welfare benefits. You will not be allowed back into the United States for *any* reason if you choose to leave. You have three clear choices; get to work, get gone, or risk getting shot if you resort to crime. Your choice!

Regarding black people, you did not arrive here as slaves, you are free people just the same as any other people who are born in the USA or are naturalized citizens. I did not bring you here, neither did my father or his father. To the able bodied white people who share the poverty and poor living conditions I say the same thing. Do not attempt to blame the current generations of people for your personal problems. Either pick yourself up, as anyone else who wants to succeed must do, and quit blaming and complaining, or lay down and do nothing and quit complaining. It is your choice, blame no one else if you have no place to live or nothing to eat. The past is a book that is finished, the past is forever closed and nothing can be done about what has happened. To waste your life living in that closed past is the single biggest mistake you can ever make, because it has no future. The future is the rest of this day and all of your tomorrows, do something with it or about it or dry on the vine. It is up to you. But don't think about becoming, or continuing to be, a criminal because you may be shot on sight when caught in the act!

The fact that The Great Society is instead a great failure is a fact and has had a forty year run as a chance to prove that it was a good idea.

Lets take a look at it on a one to one basis, a personal relationship between you and I.

If you were my next door neighbor and came upon hard times through no fault of your own, such as losing your job or because of a serious accident or health problem, I would share what I have with you to help you for a while until you could get back on your feet. I think that most Americans would do the same thing if you were their neighbor. If however you made no attempt to recover, refused to return to work or to look for work, I would at some point say "Enough is enough." If when I am going off to work I see that you are still in bed and that you are denigrating our neighborhood because you make no attempt to keep your home and car up to par with plenty of time on your hands, I am going to be very upset with you. Additionally if I come home from work and I see that you have done nothing to improve your situation, my attitude will change more. To top it off if I see that you bought food with your food stamps and saved your Social Security cash to buy beer or liquor, I will be angry . If I see that you are using and/or dealing drugs I am going to be furious! I will make it very clear to you that I will help you no more, give you no more food or money because of *your* actions. I will have had it!

It is the very same thing when all of the above conditions are identical except that the government withholds money from my paycheck , runs it through an inefficient agency so it is not so visible, shrinks it through bureaucratic waste, and sends you what is left of my money. They take my money to provide you with subsidized or free housing, electricity, and food stamps. They send my money to subsidize noncompetitive businesses, those who produce your free rice and honey and powdered milk and cheese. And you have the gall and audacity to complain about the government and hate me!

It is not only time, it is past time to rectify this cultural disaster and begin the process to turn it around. It won't be quick and it will not be easy. There are going to be some people sacrificed who are playing on the wrong side of the game in order to save people who they would harm if we don't stop the offenders.

The days when because you are young and strong you can mug someone else's mother in the street because she is old and defenseless must come to an abrupt end. You who would beat and rob old or defenseless people are despicable and should be stopped immediately with whatever amount of force is required. You who burglarize and destroy other people's property in the process need a little sample of good old time justice on the spot, meaning if you are caught and refuse to obey orders you will be shot! For this powerful nation to let it's most defenseless and vulnerable citizens to be brutalized, terrorized, robbed and killed because we are too weak to deliver swift justice to the perpetrators is a crime itself. If you support the soft on crime position *you* are partly responsible for the next rape, murder or property crime. Are you comfortable with that? Remember also that it just might be you or your family or friend next!

The current attitudes of "if you treat them nice maybe they will treat you nice in return" is responsible for much of the violence and criminal behavior rampaging through the country today. The time to start the turnaround is now.

Step number one in returning this element of our current culture to civility is to *stop supporting and rewarding bad behavior*. When people who commit crimes profit from the publicity and the notoriety of their evil deeds it is inviting more of the same. There was a time not long ago when society shunned criminals and people who were of low moral character. It was shameful to be known as a criminal or a person of low moral character and had the effect of discouraging actions that would brand and identify you as such.

It is incredible that today some criminals reap huge rewards from book sales, television royalties, become celebrities making the TV talk show circuit and become hugely rich from sales of Cds, videos and DVDs by exploiting their illegal activities. Some are even rewarded with their own TV shows featuring them as host. Starting at the bedrock level we must teach new generations that this is wrong and is destroying honesty, decency, and their civilization.

There must be an enforceable minimum of decency and respect for others in the interpretation of the First Amendment regarding *freedom of speech.* It is unthinkable that a civilized nation would allow itself to be bombarded with the filth and degrading actions and words, written and spoken, that we endure in public every day. When you are in the public these days there is no way to avoid hearing and seeing those infamous four letter words that are so offensive, repulsive and embarrassing, or the middle finger "California Salute." The words were used in the past for their shock value in extreme situations. They are used so commonly in the last few years by people of all ages that there is no real shock value left, rather disgust and loathing for the speaker by people who do not like to hear foul language. There is no way to watch commercial TV today and avoid seeing and hearing this trash, even when you think that you are safe because it is a "family" oriented show. Justin Timberlake and Janet Jackson's caper, a classic example, only served to make them more popular instead of being forever banned from any future TV broadcast. This is a terrible goal to set for young people coming up today, to say nothing of the fact that every four letter word ever invented is barely veiled or bleeped in today's run of the mill productions. Even worse is the so called "music" that is filled with any and all of the uncensored four letter words ever spoken, rap music being the classic example. You and your children are not protected from it because you can't escape it when some punk has his or her stereo pumping that filth out with the windows down and the volume at car shaking levels. And too many young people eat it up, they can't get enough of it. It lets them into the fantasy of the adult world long before they are emotionally developed enough to handle it. It is disgusting to hear little boys call eight, nine, ten year old girls "Bitches" and "Hos." What on earth have we been thinking? Where did the real men go to whom those were fighting words when used in public? Say nothing about when applied to impressionable little girls.

What has caused a country with the strongest military on earth to let violent gangs roam and rule the streets? Are freedom of speech and civil rights so overwhelmingly important that we must tolerate the horror of these well organized criminals conducting their drug empires and drug wars right in the center of our most highly populated areas, recruiting our kids, all the while proudly wearing their "colors?" If we are saying that we are going to have a "war on drugs" then let's have a *real* war. Our well trained military would wipe these punks out in a matter of weeks if we had the guts to deploy them and give them the order *shoot to kill*. We all know that there is a danger in using the military to deal with civil matters, but we are under attack, from within as well as from foreign sources outside of the country. If we can justify using the military to protect the country, which is in fact a grouping of it's individuals, then what is wrong with using it to protect a single individual? These gangs who are so violent when robbing and beating unarmed ordinary people would not think they were so "bad" if they were facing well trained military personnel with the weapons and orders to stop the violence and drug dealing on the spot with any amount of force required to do the job. That in turn would serve notice to the younger generations that this is no career to consider for fast money and an easy life with no job required. They would understand the real meaning of a *dead end* job.

It has progressed beyond the capacity of police departments to deal with, police are trained to keep the peace. Soldiers are trained to fight a war. Many of the young police officers who grew up accepting this culture as a part of life do not have the experience and seasoning to realize how severe it has become, and that there was a time when it was not allowed to exist. It will take the military with a proactive move now, or at some later time when the civil disobedience and violence grows to the point where it will be a situation requiring Marshall Law or worse.

There is some chance that a turnaround could be successful if enough committed people get involved, take a stand, and organize to demand that our elected leaders start solving these huge problems. It is not mandatory to do anything, but does any sane person think that these problems will solve themselves? Think about it for a while and then make a decision, to do what you can, or do nothing. What will the result be if the problems continue unchecked? Will you want to live in that world? Is the suggested SAFA a possible start toward some solutions?

There was an research experiment conducted many years ago where laboratory rats were subjected to two extremely different living conditions. A male and a female rat were put in a large cage with ample room to set up housekeeping and raise a family. They devised a nursery area and a separate place for their bodily waste, they kept the cage clean and organized and raised a normal healthy well adjusted family.

Another cage was filled with too many rats relative to it's size. The result was exactly the opposite of the other rat family. There was immediate fighting over territory, no sacred quarter for a nursery, no designated toilet area. The rats degenerated into filth, disease, loss of hair, homosexuality, cannibalism, mayhem and eventual massive devastation of the population. Sounds in some respects like the Super Dome in the days following Hurricane Katrina!

There is a very loud and clear message here. Can *you* hear it?

CHAPTER EIGHT
THE IMMIGRATION DISASTER

At the time of this writing the President of the United States George W. Bush, the United States Congress, and the United States Senate are attempting to make difficult decisions on the subject of our immigration problems. The problems are very complex and the outcome unknown.

Like every other problem it is simple when not confounded by special interests and politics. We are being invaded by millions of people from other countries, primarily from Mexico because of our common border. There are four entities at fault, the immigrants, the American people who provide them with jobs, the Mexican government, and the United States government.

The solution is obvious and simple; seal the borders, cut off the jobs, demand that both governments support and enforce these actions with any and all force necessary. When that is in place there must be a standard established which will determine which when and how illegals now living here will be returned to their own country. This will have to be decided by some of the same people and government agencies who allowed the problem to escalate to the current crisis level in the first place. Not a comforting thought! But remember, *if man made it,man can fix it*!

If an unknown person were to invade your personal home and threaten your security, perhaps your life and property, you would probably call the appropriate authorities, if you could. (Remember in this day and age you are in a vulnerable position if you use force to defend yourself and/or your property! What a sad state of affairs!) You could reasonably expect that the police or sheriff's department or other law enforcement officials would respond and attempt to rescue you and apprehend the intruder or intruders. Hopefully the criminals would be brought to justice. However in an almost identical situation on a massive scale there are no authorities to call who have the authority and power to stop the immigrant invasion, in most cases apprehension is a revolving door back to Mexico, and there is basically no punishment for breaking the law by entering the country illegally. The Border Patrol is overwhelmed, the National Guard will be used with it's hands tied behind it's back, other law enforcement agencies can't, or won't, because of archaic laws and the need to protect their own turf as they see it, and we don't have the stomach to effectively use the armed forces who could best do the job. But this is too simplistic, we need to confound it with special interests, politics, oh, and don't forget political correctness.

Please don't misunderstand me, I have great sympathy for some of these immigrant people. I know some of them. I have worked with them. I have respect for them. But our country is under attack, and the law is the law. Either enforce it or change it!

I have information from a one hundred percent reliable source that in the city where I live there is an eighteen year old Mexican woman and her newborn child receiving approximately $750.00 of value and/or cash every month, plus free government program foods, baby formula, milk, other dairy products and cereals. She and her husband are both here illegally, but she qualifies for all of this plus paid hospital and medical expenses for birth of the child for mother and child, twelve months free medical care for the child, and a free six month checkup for the mother. The child was born here and is automatically an American citizen. My source tells me that there are many such cases in this city, and that it is common all over the United States.

There is a scenario taking place regarding illegals who come here solely for the purpose of defrauding the system. These are not the typical meek and mild people we perceive the Mexican illegals to be. They are well coached, very vocal and demanding. The procedure goes something like this according to information circulating on the internet. I have not confirmed any of this, I am just repeating information that is available on the net, but substantiated by the preceding scenario.

#1. The very pregnant Mexican woman crosses the border into the United States illegally.

#2 She delivers the child, who is born a US citizen, all hospital and medical expenses are billed to the US Government as soon as the documents are signed. The child qualifies for twelve months free care and the mother is eligible for a six week checkup. When released from the hospital the mother may apply for the free baby food formula, dairy products and cereals provided under the WIC program.

#3 The mother can now apply for emergency food stamps for the child and receive as much as $152 a month, and if she claims that the father is living in Mexico she can apply for TANF cash assistance of up to $100 a month.

#4 If she qualifies for the TANF assistance she can now apply for free childcare from a state funded agency, also she may receive free or reduced cost public housing. From that point there are a number of programs available which provide for up to $84 a month utility assistance, school allowance, and of course free school supplies. Breakfast and lunches are provided when the child is of school age even though the family qualifies for food stamps.

#5 The mother can apply for health insurance coverage for each child, receiving up to $400 a month value of paid insurance premiums per child. Evidently she can repeat this entire process if and when other children are born.

#6 If the mother returns to Mexico to live she can continue to receive the food stamps and TANF benefits if she can cross the border to buy groceries with the food stamps and collect her TANF cash every month.

This is a snapshot of a system that is completely and totally out of control. On a family based level, our first responsibility is to provide for and protect our own family. After all, America is in essence a giant family of people, yet somehow all common sense and responsibility have been thrown out the window. How on earth did the people elected and appointed to do our business, protect us and provide some sensible safety net programs let things get so far out of hand. Does the entire economic system and the country have to collapse for it to stop, or is there still time enough before then that we can start to turn things around?

Because there is new legislation under consideration at this time, it is not appropriate to comment further until the outcome of those pending actions are known. If there is time to comment on the new laws regarding immigration problems and an opportunity to reduce the problems to simple terms with some suggestions for solutions before this goes to print I will do so. If not, there will be another publication addressing this and many other pressing social problems.

Are there enough of us with the will to take a stand and make a change?

Is America headed for a fall?

What do you think?

ABOUT THE AUTHOR

Ray Douglas is alternately a businessman and a musician/ singer/ entertainer having spent years doing both, sometimes simultaneously, sometimes separately. Both professions have brought him into close contact and relationships with many people. Sooner or later in most serious conversations the subject of the many problems facing the United States is brought up and discussed. Inevitably people ask each other for or give their opinions on the subjects that are discussed.

Naturally the opinions are wide and varied, but one stands out in virtually every conversation. People unanimously believe that the United States is headed for trouble beyond the usual politics, taxes, etc., etc.. One man put it bluntly, America is headed for a fall.

There is deep concern on many subjects; exportation of jobs, immigration problems, foreign military actions, nukes, Social Security going broke as the Baby Boomers reach retirement age to give a few examples. But there is one big overriding subject that is talked about in hushed guarded tones. It is the downward cultural spiral linked to the drug addiction and substance abuse problems in the United States and world wide. People are aware that it is raging out of control and realize that something must be done. But how?

Ray Douglas believes that it is probable that a slim majority of the American people are not actively a part of the problem. Most are contributing, however, by being passive and not taking a stand or speaking out when they observe problems. He admits to being one hundred percent guilty of this, this is his attempt to make a difference. He salutes those who have worked and sacrificed to keep America strong and on the right track. These people are excluded from the criticisms in the book.

With years to observe and think about it, Ray Douglas decided to ask one final question at or near the end of such conversations. Is America headed for a fall? The answer is virtually always the same, a resounding yes.

The result of these countless conversations and years of observation coupled with some deep concern and soul searching are the sum and substance of this book, written from one man's point of view and in one man's opinion.